catalyst groupzine™
Volume 1. Challenge the Process

Catalyst GroupZine™

Volume 1. **Challenge the Process**

Published by Nelson Impact, a Division of Thomas Nelson, Inc., P.O. Box 141000, Nashville, Tennessee, 37214.

For more information on the Catalyst Conference or to order additional copies of the Catalyst GroupZine™, call INJOY at 1-888-334-6569 or visit www.catalystconference.com.

To find out how to exhibit or be a sponsor at the Catalyst Conference, contact Stacy Coleman (stacy.coleman@injoy.com).

Design and Art Direction: FiveStone, Atlanta, Georgia (www.FiveStone.com)

Cover Photo: Jeremy Cowart Photography, Nashville, Tennessee (www.jeremycowart.com)

ISBN: 1-4185-0325-8

Printed in the United States of America.

What is Catalyst?

Catalyst exists to ignite passion for Christ and develop the leadership potential of the next generation, equipping them to engage and impact their world. Catalyst is an INJOY brand dedicated to serve, connect, and develop men and women of faith through innovative resources, events, and training.

The Catalyst Story

In 2000, Catalyst was birthed out of a handful of young leaders at INJOY and Northpoint Community Church in Atlanta, Georgia who imagined a new experience – a leadership awakening that would revolutionize Next Generation Leaders for the Kingdom of God. What began as only a vision caught fire and over the past six years, more than 35,000 young leaders have gathered for the annual Catalyst Conference (**www.catalystconference.com**).

Today Catalyst is more than a conference—it's a creative community of young leaders who are passionate about their generation and eager to learn from wise communicators, mentors, and teachers to increase their influence.

The Catalyst Vision: Revolutionize Next Generation Leaders

A revolution, by nature, is a sudden, radical and fundamental change in the organization of leadership in a socioeconomic scenario. Historically, radical underground networks have shifted existing structures in order to jolt an organization out of the grip of one dictator and place it into the hands of a new influencer.

Catalyst sees a need to ignite and unite the next generation of leaders, allowing their passions and gifts to flourish as they serve as change agents in our churches and culture. Similar to historical radicals, these next generation leaders desire to engage the world in authentic and tangible ways and are increasingly dissatisfied with status quo.

Any revolution, including those that are God-initiated, needs a place to connect and network. Catalyst sees its role as a voice and forum to gather, stir up, equip and unite this next generation of leaders with ongoing encouragement and support. Our dream is that one day, in the near future, next generation leaders would confidently and humbly embrace God's call on their lives and faithfully fulfill his commission to lead people in a way that is aligned with his heart and purpose.

The Elements of Catalyst

We believe that a Next Generation Leader is:

Uncompromising in Integrity
Passionate about God
Intentional about Community
Courageous in Calling
Engaged in Culture

Table of Elements

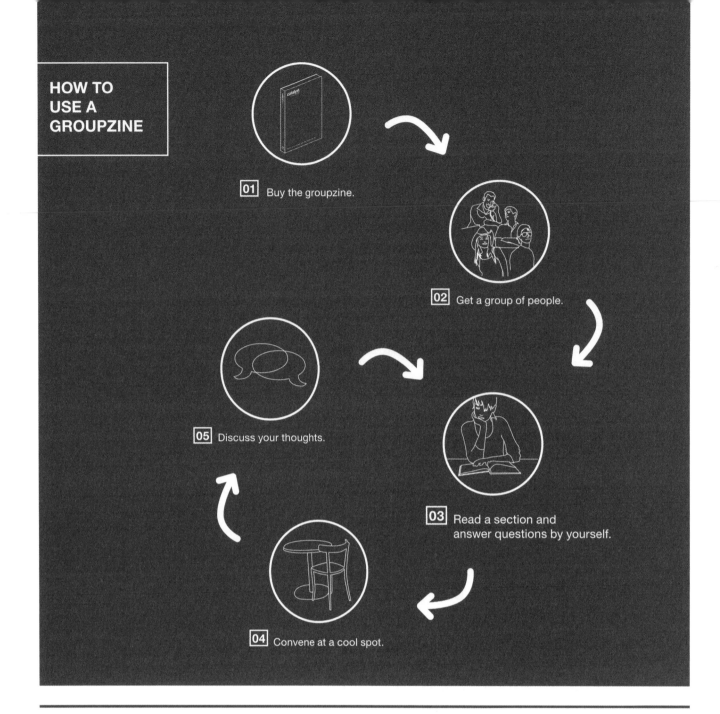

HOW TO USE A GROUPZINE

01 Buy the groupzine.

02 Get a group of people.

03 Read a section and answer questions by yourself.

04 Convene at a cool spot.

05 Discuss your thoughts.

Small Group Leaders (Read Here) . . .

The Conversation

As a small group leader, you are often expected to have all the answers . . . and let's be honest—you don't have all the answers. However, you do tend to have the most questions and the confidence to share them.

So that's how you lead: Bring your questions to the group and find the answers together. Conversation is the starting point to form true community, and through your dialogue the group will grow.

Some discussion points are provided throughout the GroupZine™, but you'll notice there is also plenty of white space to doodle, dream, and create your own questions.

The Environment

Gather your group at a coffee shop, discuss over dinner, meet in a cultural hotspot of your city, host a meeting in the church van, or even ask to use your pastor's house for one night. Mix up the environment to inspire and be a catalyst for the conversation.

For More Information

For those of you who need a little more structure for your small group setting, you can download a more detailed leader's guide from the Catalyst GroupZine™ website, **www.groupzines.com**.

To You. A Catalyst.

You desire to be a leader and so do I. As growing leaders, we see everything a bit differently from the people around us. For example, I recently sat down with a group of close friends—my community—and realized that many people see me as a critical thinker. This is a quality that can be a great strength, but also a detrimental weakness. With this gift, I intuitively look at many issues or problems and challenge them, but don't always respond and communicate in the right way. Challenging the process is something that all great leaders are naturally wired to do. But, I am learning that we need to not only challenge the ideas, but also find solutions, recommend a better path to take, and purposefully engage those around us to help re-imagine a new way. When we do this, the potential for influence to increase is exponential. Leadership is influence.

The Catalyst Team thought it would be most helpful to create a way for you and your friends, colleagues, or partners in ministry to dig deeper into the elements that make up the life of a truly influential leader. The fluid structure of the *Catalyst GroupZine*™ will challenge the way you think about traditional Bible and group study. We believe it's important for leaders to ask questions, challenge the status quo, and take risks. This format is meant to facilitate organic learning, because it creates a process for you to experience community with other revolutionaries while you engage, dialogue, debate, question, reflect, and ultimately grow.

In the weeks ahead, we will be unpacking the elements of a Catalyst leader—a person who is uncompromising in their integrity, passionate about God, intentional about community, courageous in their calling, and engaged in culture. Some of today's most influential communicators—leaders, authors and teachers have come together to provide this resource that is meant to help you and your team grow in your personal influence. You will be challenged by what you read and discuss, and I know that this study will draw you closer to God's purposes and our generation.

I pray that the elements of a Catalyst Leader resonate with your heart, mind, and soul. In your own Catalyst community, we hope you will debate them as much as we do; as this is how we have have learned, grown and built the best of relationships, ones that will continue to shape us all into influential leaders.

Your friend,

J.H

Jeff Shinabarger
jeff@catalystgroupzine.com

Thank you.
From Jeff Shinabarger

Kevin Small — for your ideation, vision, and leadership
Wayne Kinde and *Les Middleton* — for believing in a new concept
Jason Locy – for a beautiful creation
Gabe Lyons – for teaming with me, while teaching me
Kerry Priest – for commitment through this process
Brad Lomenick – for the opportunity to create this project
André Jean – Te amo mi amor

Special thanks also to:
Dennis Worden, Reggie Goodin, Mark Cole, Mack Kitchel, Chad Johnson, Mandy Campbell, Beth Nelson, Natalie Carlson, Abby Johnson, Matthew Berry, Melissa Kruse, Julie Cramer, Becky Kruse, Patricio Juarez, Ben Ortlip and all our contributors.

catalyst
GROUPZINE ™

Volume 1. Challenge the Process

Catalyst
PO Box 7700
Atlanta, GA 30357
www.injoy.com
www.catalystgroupzine.com

Executive Editor
Jeff Shinabarger

Associate Editor
Brad Lomenick

Managing Editor
Kerry Priest

Contributing Editor
Tim Willard

Design and Art Direction
FiveStone.com

Cover Photo
Jeremy Cowart

Contributing Writers:
Andy Stanley
Ben Ortlip
Brian McLaren
Bryan Davidson
Christine Willard
David Crowder
Donald Miller
Ron Martoia
Elisa Morgan
Erwin McManus
Howard Hendricks
Jason Locy
Jeff Shinabarger
John Eldredge
John C. Maxwell
Kevin Myers
Kyle Lake
Louie Giglio
Margaret Feinberg
Mark Sanborn
Melissa Kruse
Mike Yankoski
Nancy Pearcey
Rick McKinley
Rick Packer
Stanley Grenz
Tim Elmore
Tim Willard
Valorie Burton

Consultants:
Michael and Hayley Dimarco, Hungry Planet
Dr. Stephen R. Graves, Cornerstone Group
Bill Donahue, Willow Creek Church
Gabe Lyons

If you have a story idea, questions, feedback, or would like to submit a TRUE STORY profile for the next Catalyst GroupZine™, email us *groupzines@injoy.com*. For information on the Catalyst Conference visit us online at *www.catalystconference.com*. To purchase other INJOY or Catalyst resources call 1-800-333-6506.

AUTHENTIC in Influence

How do I lead others?

Leadership is influence. I am not a leader if others are not following. Influence can't be forced or contrived. It can only be won over time. If I am living out the five elements of a Catalyst Leader, influence will be natural, compelling and attractive. If not, it will be challenged by others and ineffective.

b. 01

b. 02

b. 03

THE INSTINCT TO CHALLENGE THE PROCESS IS A FUNDAMENTAL QUALITY OF EVERY LEADER. WHEN GOD CREATED LEADERS, HE EQUIPPED THEM WITH AN UNSETTLING URGE TO UNPACK, UNDO, AND UNEARTH METHODS. THIS EXPLAINS YOUR TENDENCY TO QUESTION EVERYTHING AROUND YOU. IT'S THE REASON YOU HAVE SUCH STRONG OPINIONS – AND SUCH A STRONG DESIRE TO SHARE THEM. GOD WIRED YOU THAT WAY.

b. 04

figure 30.

CHALLENGE THE PROCESS
DEFYING THE GRAVITATIONAL PULL OF THE STATUS QUO

By Andy Stanley

I'VE NEVER BEEN ONE TO TAKE THE OBVIOUS PATH. WHEN I WAS A TEENAGER, MY FATHER GAVE ME THE SIMPLE JOB OF STACKING SOME FIREWOOD AS HE LEFT FOR WORK ONE DAY. OF COURSE THERE WAS A PART OF ME THAT RESISTED FACING SUCH A LABOR-INTENSIVE JOB; BUT EVEN STRONGER WAS THE PART OF ME THAT RESISTED DOING IT IN AN ORDINARY WAY. SO AS I STARTED MOVING THE WOOD AROUND, I WAS GRADUALLY OVERCOME BY A DESIRE TO CREATE SOMETHING THAT HAD NEVER BEEN DONE BEFORE. WHAT SHOULD HAVE BEEN A MUNDANE CHORE SOON BECAME A QUEST. FOR HOURS I STACKED AND RESTACKED, CULTIVATING THE VISION IN MY MIND. BY THE TIME MY FATHER RETURNED HOME, HE WAS GREETED BY A MASTERPIECE THAT SURPRISED (AND PROBABLY BAFFLED) HIM.

figure 6 c.

CHALLENGE THE PROCESS

I think there's something in every leader that yearns to try things in new ways, to test the status quo – to challenge the process. If you're a leader, you've probably had similar experiences all your life. Leaders are constantly evaluating and critiquing the world around us. When most people are moved by a message, we leaders are busy examining the structure of the presentation. Where the average person enjoys a great conference, we're fixated on the methods that made it successful. There's something in every leader that seeks to understand – to celebrate and to improve – the process at work behind the scenes.

The rest of the world is quite the opposite. In fact, it's human nature to gravitate toward the familiar. Left to themselves, virtually every person and organization is in a subconscious pursuit of a status quo. Eventually they will find it. And they will work very, very hard to stay there.

Consider this quote from *The Leadership Challenge*: "Leaders must challenge the process precisely because any system will unconsciously conspire to maintain the status quo and prevent change. It is the nature of things organizationally not to change in a healthy direction. It is the nature of things organizationally to find a happy place and stay there forever and ever and ever and ever."

In a changing world, familiar is no measure of effectiveness. And the status quo is no benchmark for long-term achievement. That's why the world needs leaders to venture boldly into the unfamiliar and to embrace the uncomfortable—because the best solutions are often found in unfamiliar, uncomfortable places.

The instinct to challenge the process is a fundamental quality of every leader. When God created leaders, he equipped them with an unsettling urge to unpack, undo, and unearth methods. This explains your tendency to question everything around you. It's the reason you have such strong opinions—and such a strong desire to share them. God wired you that way. Deep in your heart you may feel that if you were in charge, things would not only be different, they'd be better. This is not a problem of arrogance or pride. It's simply the way God wired you. It's a good thing.

Unfortunately, your zeal for improvement isn't always appreciated out in the real world. As a matter of fact, your natural bent for leadership sets you up for resistance from virtually all sides—including other leaders. And unless you understand the nature of these dynamics, the very instincts that qualify you for greatness can also lead you to disqualify yourself and sabotage your opportunities. Effective leadership means learning to challenge the process without challenging the organization. There's a fine line between the two. But it's a crucial line.

The first line of resistance the leader faces is the organization itself. As we've already mentioned, organizations don't like new ideas. It's enough of a challenge just figuring out the old ones. So the last thing an organization wants is someone suggesting that we need to start all over again with a different process. Your supervisors, advisors, elders, deacons, and staff all feel pretty much the same way. Since human nature is to seek a place of equilibrium, change is seen as a disruption of progress.

The second line of resistance you face is from other leaders. You might think you'd find an advocate in this group. But by nature, when you challenge a concept, you challenge the conceiver. You don't mean it that way, but that can be how it's often perceived. Many talented leaders have "led" themselves right out of a job because their desire to challenge the process was misunderstood, or perhaps even threatening, to those in charge. While on the other side of the spectrum, many skilled leaders have resigned themselves to conform to the status quo, squelching and squashing their natural instincts because there's no obvious opportunity to be who God made them to be.

As leaders, we must keep a sense of diplomacy without shrinking from our scrutinizing nature. When you stop challenging the process, you cease to be a leader and you become a manager. There's nothing wrong with managers. The world needs those too, but it's a different job description from the leader's. And if you cease to challenge, then you have abdicated your true calling and giftedness in the world.

"LEADERS MUST CHALLENGE THE PROCESS PRECISELY BECAUSE ANY SYSTEM WILL UNCONSCIOUSLY CONSPIRE TO MAINTAIN THE STATUS QUO AND PREVENT CHANGE. IT IS THE NATURE OF THINGS ORGANIZATIONALLY NOT TO CHANGE IN A HEALTHY DIRECTION. IT IS THE NATURE OF THINGS ORGANIZATIONALLY TO FIND A HAPPY PLACE AND STAY THERE FOREVER AND EVER AND EVER AND EVER." *p. 12*

quoted from *The Leadership Challenge*

Successful leaders must learn how to alienate a process without alienating the people who created it, or the people who work it faithfully every day.

So exactly how can you exercise your instinct to challenge, yet stay out of trouble with your superiors and those that God has placed in authority over you? As a Christian leader committed to seeing the local church advance and make progress, what exactly should you do with all this?

Here are five suggestions to help you develop the art of challenging the process without inadvertently issuing a challenge to the people in your organization.

1. When an instruction is given, follow through now; debrief later

When the discussion's over and somebody looks at you and they're clearly the authority that God has placed over you and they say, "This is what we're gonna do," then you do it. Follow through first, and debrief later. Or, as we taught our young children to say, "Yes, sir, Daddy. Why?" You see, on one hand I want them to be able to ask questions in our home. I don't want them to grow up doing everything just because, "My daddy told me to." At the same time, I want them to grow up with the security of knowing that they have parents who assume the positions of authority for the family. In other words, I want to ensure that they're committed to obedience first; and then we can talk about anything they want to. It's not simply, "Why?" It's, "Yes, sir, Daddy. Why?" "Yes, sir, Mommy. Why?"

It's the same way in your job. Your words and actions need to express, "I am clearly and squarely on your team and under your authority." It doesn't mean you can't ask, "Why?" But you do so in the clear context of serving the organization at large and observing the chain-of-command perpetually. And in your own style and your own way, you must learn to communicate both: "I am under your authority. Can we talk about it?"

2. Never verbalize your frustration[fn 12] with the process in front of other team members

There's an incredible principle behind this suggestion: "Loyalty publicly results in leverage privately." If you want to have leverage one-on-one with your authorities, then show support for his or her ideas and strategies in front of the team—even if you think they're absolutely off the wall. Likewise, if you want to lose leverage with your boss, then disrupt and ask challenging questions and foster division among the ranks publicly. Support publicly; challenge privately. Reverse those two things and you surrender your authority as a leader within your organization.

Again, it's okay to think different, and it's okay to challenge. But the method you use, and the place you choose is critical. Everybody who has authority is also under authority. So consequently, we have to learn to walk that fine line—not shrinking back from challenging, but at the same time not challenging in the wrong way and subsequently losing our leverage with those that we hope to influence and bring about change and progress.

3. Don't confuse your insights with moral imperatives[fn 12]

For the sake of argument, let's assume you are the smartest person in your church. You understand ministry like no one else. Between the two of us, you represent the model of how all churches will operate in the enlightened future. But meanwhile, let's suppose your pastor calls a meeting with the board to review their plans for the upcoming season. As expected, they produce several of the absolute worst ideas you could imagine. That's not the way to reach students. That's not the way to deal with choir. That's not the way to lead worship. That's not the way to structure the evangelism program. Needless to say, your ideas are better, more relevant, more effective, cooler, more fun, cheaper, and would reach more lost people for Christ.

Even if you're sure you've been given a superior view of the world, that doesn't mean it's a moral imperative that everyone executes your plan. In other words, if you don't do it your way, you haven't sinned. Believe it or not, there's actually something more important than doing ministry the most relevant, cool, and effective way. All that is important, but first, God is interested in seeing us learn to live and lead under the authority that God has placed over us. Your awesome ideas that you are sure will work are not moral imperatives. You have not sinned by doing ministry ineffectively. You have not sinned by simply taking the marching orders from somebody who's not as smart as you and doing things that aren't as effective as you would like to have done them.

Sometimes when leaders are geared up and passionate about an area of ministry, there's a temptation to justify flat-out rebellion for the sake of the mission and the cause. God has you where He has you for a purpose. On one hand you can't shut down your leadership instincts. But on the other hand, you can't work against the authority God has placed over you. God is using you not only to do your current ministry, but also to prepare you for whatever else He has for you. And learning to challenge the process while staying under authority is part of the lesson. And that's never a waste of time. Even if you never see your ideas implemented, you've had a good day as a leader when you've done everything you can to challenge while staying under the authority that God has placed over you. Furthermore, you will have taken a step in preparation for whatever God is leading you to accomplish in the future.

4. If you don't learn to lead under,[k. 12] you probably won't have as many opportunities to lead over

Your ability to lead others is directly related to your ability to follow others. Acknowledging authority means recognizing what it means to be responsible as well as what it means to be accountable. It's not simply one or the other. The principle of authority is a dynamic that flows in both directions. Since God is the giver and the head of all authority, all people in an organization's chain of command—leaders and followers – must ultimately answer to God. So when you sign up to participate in authority, you automatically ascribe to the concept of following. As a result, your ability to lead will never far exceed your ability to follow.

One of my favorite stories in the life of Jesus is His encounter with a Centurion whose servant was sick. The Centurion had been watching Jesus and seen Him perform miracles and heal people. So like many others who approached Jesus for help, he knew Jesus had the power to heal. However, as a member of the Roman army, he brought an amazing perspective to the situation. The Centurion didn't approach Jesus saying, "Jesus, clearly You're in charge, clearly You are an authority—therefore, would You come heal my servant who's sick?" Instead, He notices that Jesus is, "A man under authority." Based on that observation, He considers Jesus qualified to invoke healing power on His sick servant.

figure 6 c.

What a brilliant insight. I think most of us would have said, "Jesus, since You can speak to demons and demons leave, and since You can speak to illness and illness goes away, please use some of your authority for my situation." But the Centurion understood this principle. So his natural way of expressing it was to note that since Jesus possessed authority, he must also be under authority. As he explains, he knows what it's like to stand in front of a hundred men and give them orders and see them obey. And he knew their reason for obeying was not based on him, but based on the fact that he represented Rome's authority. He had authority because he was under Rome's authority. This one brief encounter illustrates such n incredible principle for those of us who are leaders. In order to have authority, you must be under authority. Because every authority is under authority.

You see, so often God is about the task of training and preparing leaders to have greater authority later in life. Consequently, we must be under authority throughout the process.

Needless to say, that creates a natural sense of conflict. As leaders, we must challenge the process; but we must also work with the authorities that God has placed over us. And we dare not upset His plan for us by rebelling against the ones God has placed over us—whether intentionally or unintentionally.

5. When you can't follow, then it's time to get off the team

The question young leaders ask me more than any other question is, "How do I know when it's time to go?" There's no simple answer to that question. But I know that for every leader, eventually the time will come when God is going to lead you to become part of another team. One of the catalysts for moving on is when staying in your current environment ceases to be a growing experience and starts to become a dying experience. Sometimes it's hard to tell which is which. But in the process of trying to challenge and lobbying for change, eventually you can begin to feel like you're no longer growing, but are dying on the inside. You may feel like you just can't bear to stay in the environment any longer. When that time comes, it's time to go. If you're not careful, you can stay so long that you become cynical and critical, and it's difficult not to breed dissension.

If you start to have those feelings, it's a good idea to ask yourself if God might be prompting you to move on. There comes a time to get off the team. If you aren't listening carefully, you could expose yourself and others to temptations you'd rather avoid. Don't give opportunity for frustration or anger to lead you. Allow God to lead you in His time to do whatever else He has for you. **C**

Andy Stanley is a graduate of Dallas Theological Seminary and is the founding pastor of North Point Community Church (**www.northpoint.org**) in Atlanta, Georgia, with a youthful congregation of more than 12,000 he is the bestselling author of *Visioneering, The Next Generation Leader, The Best Question Ever,* and *How Good Is Good Enough?*. Andy and his wife, Sandra have two sons and a daughter.

FOR GROUP DISCUSSION

Use these questions and journal pages to reflect and respond to what you've just read.

1 *When was the first time you realized God had created you to "challenge the process?" Give examples.*

2 *In the real world, are you more likely to shy away from this God–given instinct or to burst with passion to the extent of over-challenging others?*

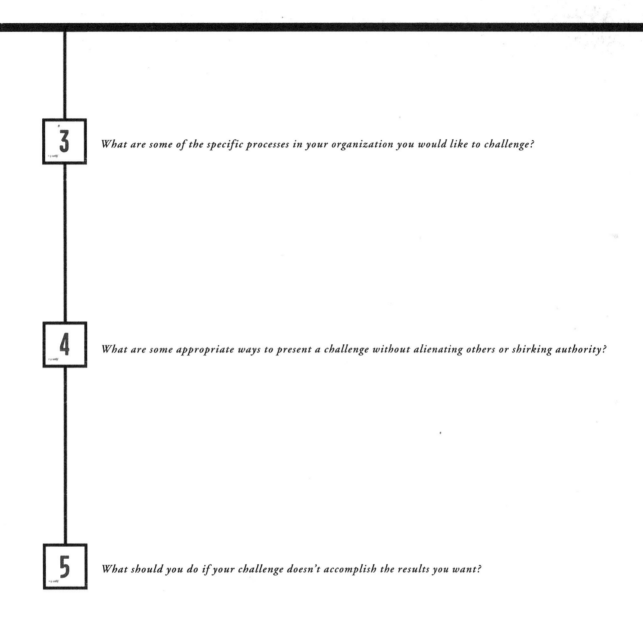

3   *What are some of the specific processes in your organization you would like to challenge?*

4   *What are some appropriate ways to present a challenge without alienating others or shirking authority?*

5   *What should you do if your challenge doesn't accomplish the results you want?*

DEEP DIVE
Download a complete smallgroup leader's guide at **www.catalystgroupzine.com**

For more information on the story of Jesus and the Centurion, check
out Matthew 8:5-13.

TRUE STORY

Earn the Ear of Others

MOHAN ZACHARIAH

Mohan Zachariah leads a staff of sixteen at Mission Year in Chicago, Illinois (**www.missionyear.com**). As president of this organization that places one-year volunteers in poor communities around the U.S., Mohan carries the vision for Mission Year. But he's quick to point out that he's not the only influencer of that vision. "I need to hear from people about what they think," he says. "It is in the exchange of actually listening to others and my openness to act when appropriate that I am able to gain an ear of others in order to influence them."

Mohan not only articulates the vision for his organization, he has a vision for each of his staff members as well. "I think God has a vision for all of us," he states. "I try and cast that vision for what I see for their lives and how they can help meet the mission we are on." Mohan is proactive in approaching staff members about their jobs, listening to their perception of the organization, recognizing their need to be engaged on a level that goes beyond their assigned tasks. With dialogues like this, Mohan's staff ends up knowing themselves better, and they are better able to "take on challenges according to their abilities," advice Mohan gives any Next Generation Leader.

Mohan's journey to become president of Mission Year wasn't your typical career path. His journey began in the kitchen, packing sandwiches to pass out to the homeless he saw day after day on Chicago Avenue while commuting to his job at the American Bar Association. At the time, he was studying Scripture and was "overwhelmed with the amount of emphasis there was to injustice and the plight of the poor." Soon he began venturing out into the streets at night "to spend time with the homeless in order to build relationships and try to make a difference."

Later, God used a short-term missions trip to the red-light district of Mumbai, India to lead both Mohan and his wife to commit themselves to ministry among the poor. Leaving behind his career with attorneys, Mohan found the ministry at Mission Year to be closely aligned with this newfound commitment, that of using his gifts to serve the poor. Today, this dedicated husband and father is still building relationships and making a difference—as he leads a vibrant organization and mentors a younger generation of leaders. **C**

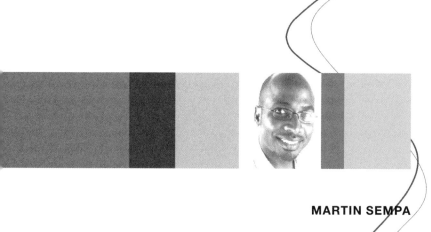

TRUE STORY

MARTIN SEMPA

The Challenge of Abstinence

Martin Sempa lives in a world surrounded by college students—young men and women whose very lives are threatened by the tragedy of HIV/AIDS in their country of Uganda. Martin, a Ugandan evangelist and church planter, believes God has called him to reach these young people with the life-saving challenge of abstinence.

"Every day I wake up thinking that there will be 700 new HIV/AIDS infections today, mostly among the 15 to 25-year-olds," he says. Martin himself has lost a sister and brother to HIV/AIDS and realizes he should have died, except for his salvation and the godly influence of one exhorting him to live a sexually pure life.

But Martin realizes he cannot do it alone. He senses that a greater impact could be made in the lives of college students if he duplicates himself. So he's developing leaders, one small group of 13 at a time—spending time mentoring and empowering them in the gospel, hoping, he says, "that they will go further and do greater than I have ever done." The emerging revival he is witnessing on the campus of Makerere University in Uganda's capital of Kampala confirms in his mind the necessity of developing new leaders. "Any movement which is not developing new leaders will become a monument of its past." On this campus of 30,000 students, Martin planted a church where 1,000 students now worship (**www.emakereoye.com**).

Martin's strong leadership skills, however, are not self-made. Martin keeps himself internally stable and strong by daily feeding on God's Word, reading through the Bible chronologically, then meditating on his reading. God has used the lives of strong leaders to speak to Martin in areas of courage, opposition, and purpose. He lists the biographies of Hudson Taylor, Alexander Mackay, and David Livingstone, along with authors such as Richard Lovelace (*Dynamics of Spiritual Life*) and Rick Warren (*The Purpose-Driven Church* and *The Purpose-Driven Life*) as being influential in his life.

Martin's prayer is that God would use him to ignite a spiritual uprising on college campuses throughout Africa, tapping into their energy to produce change and transformation in the lives of the lost, "lighting up dark Africa and the ever-darkening northern hemisphere." To God be the glory! **C**

GENNARINO DESTEFANO

TRUE STORY

Discipleship ... On Your Turf

Gennarino Destefano knows where true discipleship takes place. If you were being discipled by Gennarino, it's more likely he would hang out with you on your turf, or invite you to his home, than he would be playing the role of Bible teacher in a Sunday School class at church. "I find that real discipleship comes in the hands-on approach I use in the trenches," he relates, pointing out that a significant portion of Christ's ministry was spent "working and living directly with the twelve disciples."

Gennarino, Assistant Pastor at Calvary Chapel Fort Lauderdale (**www.calvaryftl.org**), hasn't always understood the impact of this type of influence on young men. This New York native lived a life apart from God for the first 30 years of his life, then "ran into Jesus Christ" at the church where he has been serving on staff now for more than fifteen years. From growing marijuana to growing disciples, Gennarino's life has undergone significant changes. "I simply and consistently lived obedient to what God daily set before me, watching His plan unfold." God revealed to Gennarino his life's purpose and passion—discipleship—and his ministry hasn't been the same since.

One of the greatest keys to discipleship and influence that Gennarino has uncovered while serving at the church is that "high contact leads to high impact." That explains why he singles out young men on fire for the Lord, inviting them to his home where, under the influence of Gennarino and his wife, Margaret, significant moments of discipleship are played out in the midst of life's routines. "Our more effective moments of ministry have come over coffee and laundry, rather than in the formal Bible study times."

Rewarding? You bet! "There is no greater reward for me on this side of heaven than watching these young men in whom I have invested advance in the ministry." Influencing through one-on-one discipleship—that's where you'll find Gennarino these days. **C**

YOUR STORY

Leadership is influence. Who has had the greatest influence on your life? What is a unique quality you have learned from this person that you desire to implement in your own leadership style? What will be your story of influence?

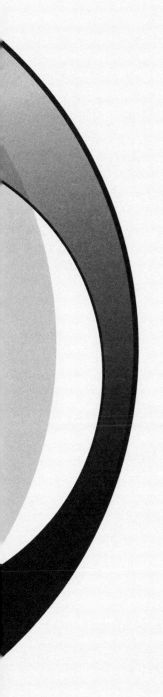

INFLUENCE

Nothing More, Nothing Less

BY JOHN C. MAXWELL

If you don't have influence, you will never be able to lead others. So how do you measure influence? Here's a story to answer that question. In late summer of 1997, people were jolted by two events that occurred less than a week apart: the deaths of Princess Diana and Mother Teresa. On the surface, the two women could not have been more different. One was a tall, young, glamorous princess from England who circulated in the highest society. The other, a Nobel Peace Prize recipient, was a small, elderly Catholic nun born in Albania, who served the poorest of the poor in Calcutta, India.

What's incredible is that their impact was remarkably similar. In a 1996 poll published by the London Daily Mail, Princess Diana and Mother Teresa were voted in first and second places as the world's two most caring people. That's something that doesn't happen unless you have a lot of influence. How did someone like Diana come to be regarded in the same way as Mother Teresa? The answer is that she demonstrated the power of the Law of Influence.

DIANA CAPTURED THE WORLD'S IMAGINATION

In 1981, Diana became the most talked-about person on the globe when she married Prince Charles of England. Nearly 1 billion people watched Diana's wedding ceremony televised from St. Paul's Cathedral. And since that day, it seemed people never could get enough news about her.

People were intrigued with Diana, a commoner who had once been a kindergarten teacher. At first she seemed painfully shy and totally overwhelmed by all the attention she and her new husband were receiving. Early in their marriage, some reports stated that Diana wasn't very happy performing the duties expected of her as a royal princess. However, in time she adjusted to her new role. As she started traveling and representing the royal family around the world at various functions, she quickly made it her goal to serve others and raise funds for numerous charitable causes. And during the process, she built many important relationships—with politicians, organizers of humanitarian causes, entertainers, and heads of state. At first, she was simply a spokesperson and catalyst for fund-raising, but as time went by, her influence increased—and so did her ability to make things happen.

Diana started rallying people to causes such as AIDS research, care for people with leprosy, and a ban on land mines. She was quite influential in bringing that last issue to the attention of the world's leaders. On a visit to the United States just months before her death,

she met with members of the Clinton administration to convince them to support the Oslo conference banning the devices. And a few weeks later, they made changes in their position. Patrick Fuller of the British Red Cross said, "The attention she drew to the issue influenced Clinton. She put the issue on the world agenda, there's no doubt about that."

THE EMERGENCE OF A LEADER

In the beginning, Diana's title had merely given her a platform to address others, but she soon became a person of influence in her own right. In 1996 when she was divorced from Prince Charles, she lost her title, but that loss didn't at all diminish her impact on others. Instead, her influence continued to increase while that of her former husband and in-laws declined—despite their royal titles and position. Why? Diana instinctively understood the Law of Influence.

Ironically, even in death Diana continued to influence others. When her funeral was broadcast on television and BBC Radio, it was translated into forty-four languages. NBC estimated that the total audience numbered as many as 2.5 billion people—more than twice the number of people who watched her wedding.

> "YOU HAVE ACHIEVED EXCELLENCE AS A LEADER WHEN PEOPLE WILL FOLLOW YOU EVERYWHERE IF ONLY OUT OF CURIOSITY."
>
> —Colin Powell

THE QUESTION OF LEADERSHIP

Princess Diana has been characterized in many ways. But one word that I've never heard used to describe her is leader. Yet that's what she was. Ultimately, she made things happen because she was an influencer, and leadership is influence—nothing more, nothing less.

LEADERSHIP IS NOT

People have so many misconceptions about leadership. When they hear that someone has an impressive title or an assigned leadership position, they assume that he is a leader. Sometimes that's true. But titles don't have much value when it comes to leading. True leadership cannot be awarded, appointed, or assigned. It comes only from influence, and that can't be mandated. It must be earned. The only thing a title can buy is a little time—either to increase your level of influence with others or to erase it.

FIVE MYTHS ABOUT LEADERSHIP

There are plenty of misconceptions and myths that people embrace about leaders and leadership. Here are five common ones:

1. THE MANAGEMENT MYTH

A widespread misunderstanding is that leading and managing are one and the same. Up until a few years ago, books that claimed to be on leadership were often really about management. The main difference between the two is that leadership is about influencing people to follow, while management focuses on maintaining systems and processes. As former Chrysler chairman and CEO Lee Iacocca wryly commented, "Sometimes even the best manager is like the little boy with the big dog, waiting to see where the dog wants to go so that he can take him there."

The best way to test whether a person can lead rather than just manage is to ask him to create positive change. Managers can maintain direction, but they can't change it. To move people in a new direction, you need influence.

2. THE ENTREPRENEUR MYTH

Frequently, people assume that all salespeople and entrepreneurs are leaders. But that's not always the case. You may remember the Ronco commercials that appeared on television years ago. They sold items such as the Veg-O-Matic, Pocket Fisherman, and Inside-the-Shell Egg Scrambler. Those products were the brainchildren of an entrepreneur named Ron Popeil. Called the salesman of the century, he has also appeared in numerous infomercials for products such as spray-on relief for baldness and food dehydrating devices.

Popeil is certainly enterprising, innovative, and successful, especially if you measure him by the $300 million in sales his products have earned. But that doesn't make him a leader. People may be buying what he has to sell, but they're not following him. At best, he is able to persuade people for a moment, but he holds no long-term influence with them.

3. THE KNOWLEDGE MYTH

Sir Francis Bacon said, "Knowledge is power." Most people, believing power is the essence of leadership, naturally assume that those who possess knowledge and intelligence are leaders. But that isn't automatically true. You can visit any major university and meet brilliant research scientists and philosophers whose ability to think is so high that it's off the charts, but whose ability to lead is so low that it doesn't even register on the charts. IQ doesn't necessarily equate to leadership.

4. THE PIONEER MYTH

Another misconception is that anyone who is out in front of the crowd is a leader. But being first isn't always the same as leading. For example, Sir Edmund Hillary was the first man to reach the summit of Mount Everest. Since his historic ascent in 1953, many people have "followed" him in achieving that feat. But that doesn't make Hillary a leader. He wasn't even the leader on that particular expedition. John Hunt was. And when Hillary traveled to the South Pole in 1958 as part of

the Commonwealth Trans-Antarctic Expedition, he was accompanying another leader, Sir Vivian Fuchs. To be a leader, a person has to not only be out front, but also have people intentionally coming behind him, following his lead, and acting on his vision.

5. THE POSITION MYTH

As mentioned earlier, the greatest misunderstanding about leadership is that people think it is based on position, but it's not. Stanley Huffty affirmed, "It's not the position that makes the leader; it's the leader that makes the position."

Look at what happened several years ago at Cordiant, the advertising agency formerly known as Saatchi & Saatchi. In 1994, institutional investors at Saatchi & Saatchi forced the board of directors to dismiss Maurice Saatchi, the company's CEO. What was the result? Several executives followed him out. So did many of the company's largest accounts, including British Airways and Mars, the candy maker. Saatchi's influence was so great that his departure caused the company's stock to fall immediately from $85 to $4 per share. What happened is a result of the Law of Influence. Saatchi lost his title and position, but he continued to be the leader.

> ## "IT'S NOT THE POSITION THAT MAKES THE LEADER; IT'S THE LEADER THAT MAKES THE POSITION."
>
> -Stanley Huffty

WHO'S THE REAL LEADER?

I personally learned the Law of Influence when I accepted my first job out of college at a small church in rural Indiana. I went in with all the right credentials. I was hired as the senior pastor, which meant that I possessed the position and title of leader in that organization. I had the proper college degree. I had even been ordained. In addition, I had been trained by my father who was an excellent pastor and a very high-profile leader in the denomination. It made for a good-looking résumé—but it didn't make me a leader. At my first board meeting, I quickly found out who was the real leader of that church. By the time I took my next position three years later, I had learned the Law of Influence. I recognized that hard work was required to gain influence in any organization and to earn the right to become the leader.

LEADERSHIP IS . . .

Leadership is influence—nothing more, nothing less. When you become a student of leaders, as I am, you recognize people's level of influence in everyday situations all around you. Let me give you an example. In 1997, I moved to Atlanta, Georgia. In that same year, Dan Reeves became the coach of the NFL's Atlanta Falcons. I was glad to hear that. Reeves is an excellent coach and leader. Though he had most recently coached the New York Giants, Reeves made his reputation as the head coach of the Denver Broncos. From 1981 to 1992, he compiled an excellent 117-79-1 record, earned three Super Bowl appearances, and received NFL Coach of the Year honors three times.

Despite Reeves's success in Denver, he didn't always experience smooth sailing. He was known to have had disagreements with quarterback John Elway and assistant coach Mike Shanahan. What was the reason for the problem? It was said that during the 1989 season, Shanahan and Elway sometimes worked on their own offensive game plan, ignoring Reeves's wishes. I don't know if that was true, but if it was, then Shanahan, not Reeves, had developed greater influence with the Denver quarterback. It didn't matter that Reeves held the title and position of head coach. It didn't even matter how good a coach Reeves was. Shanahan had become the more influential leader in the quarterback's life. And leadership is influence.

Shanahan left the Broncos at the end of that season, but he returned in 1995 as the team's head coach. He became in title what he evidently already had been in terms of influence to some of the players: their leader. And that leadership has now paid off. In January of 1998, he led the Denver Broncos franchise and quarterback John Elway to their first Super Bowl victory.

LEADERSHIP WITHOUT LEVERAGE

I admire and respect the leadership of my good friend Bill Hybels, the senior pastor of Willow Creek Community Church in South Barrington, Illinois, the largest church in North America. Bill says he believes that the church is the most leadership-intensive enterprise in society. A lot of businesspeople I know are surprised when they hear that statement, but I think Bill is right. What is the basis of his belief? Positional leadership doesn't work in volunteer organizations. Because a leader doesn't have leverage—or influence—he is ineffective. In other organizations, the person who has position has incredible leverage. In the military, leaders can use rank and, if all else fails, throw people into the brig. In business, bosses have tremendous leverage in the form of salary, benefits, and perks. Most followers are pretty cooperative when their livelihood is at stake.

But in voluntary organizations, such as churches, the only thing that works is leadership in its purest form. Leaders have only their influence to aid them. And as Harry A. Overstreet observed, "The very essence of all power to influence lies in getting the other person to participate." Followers in voluntary organizations cannot be forced to get on board. If the leader has no influence with them, then they won't follow. When I recently shared that observation with a group of about 150 CEOs from the automobile industry, I saw lightbulbs going on all over the room. And when I gave them a piece of advice, they really got excited. I'm going to share that same advice with you: If you are a businessperson and you really want to find out whether your people are capable of leading, send them out to volunteer their time in the community. If they can get people to follow them while they're serving at the Red Cross, a United Way shelter, or their local church, then you know that they really do have influence—and leadership ability.

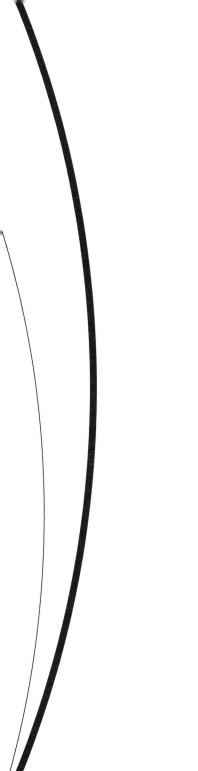

FROM COMMANDER TO PRIVATE TO COMMANDER IN CHIEF

One of my favorite stories that illustrates the Law of Influence concerns Abraham Lincoln. In 1832, years before he became president, young Lincoln gathered together a group of men to fight in the Black Hawk War. In those days, the person who put together a volunteer company for the militia often became its leader and assumed a commanding rank. In this instance, Lincoln had the rank of captain.

But Lincoln had a problem. He knew nothing about soldiering. He had no prior military experience, and he knew nothing about tactics. He had trouble remembering the simplest military procedures. For example, one day Lincoln was marching a couple of dozen men across a field and needed to guide them through a gate into another field. But he couldn't manage it. Recounting the incident later, Lincoln said, "I could not for the life of me remember the proper word of command for getting my company endwise. Finally, as we came near [the gate] I shouted: 'This company is dismissed for two minutes, when it will fall in again on the other side of the gate.'"

As time went by, Lincoln's level of influence with others in the militia actually decreased. While other officers proved themselves and gained rank, Lincoln found himself going in the other direction. He began with the title and position of captain, but that did him little good. He couldn't overcome the Law of Influence. By the end of his military service, Abraham Lincoln found his rightful place, having achieved the rank of private.

Fortunately for Lincoln—and for the fate of our country—he overcame his inability to influence others. He followed his time in the military with undistinguished stints in the Illinois state legislature and the U.S. House of Representatives. But over time and with much effort and personal experience, he became a person of remarkable influence and impact.

Here is my favorite leadership proverb: "He who thinks he leads, but has no followers, is only taking a walk." If you can't influence others, they won't follow you. And if they won't follow, you're not a leader. That's the Law of Influence. No matter what anybody else tells you, remember that leadership is influence—nothing more, nothing less. **C**

John C. Maxwell speaks to hundreds of thousands of people each year. He is the author of more than thirty books, including the best-selling *The 21 Irrefutable Laws of Leadership.* Look for his newest title, *25 Ways to Win with People*, a follow-up to *Winning With People* that highlights twenty-five specific actions for building great people skills. For more information visit **www.injoy.com**.

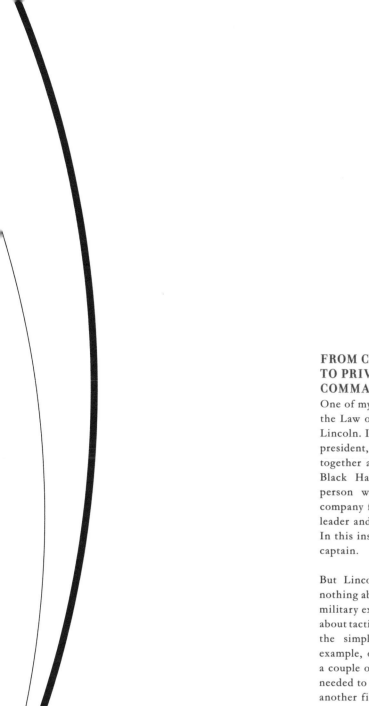

FROM COMMANDER TO PRIVATE TO COMMANDER IN CHIEF

One of my favorite stories that illustrates the Law of Influence concerns Abraham Lincoln. In 1832, years before he became president, young Lincoln gathered together a group of men to fight in the Black Hawk War. In those days, the person who put together a volunteer company for the militia often became its leader and assumed a commanding rank. In this instance, Lincoln had the rank of captain.

But Lincoln had a problem. He knew nothing about soldiering. He had no prior military experience, and he knew nothing about tactics. He had trouble remembering the simplest military procedures. For example, one day Lincoln was marching a couple of dozen men across a field and needed to guide them through a gate into another field. But he couldn't manage it. Recounting the incident later, Lincoln said, "I could not for the life of me remember the proper word of command for getting my company endwise. Finally, as we came near [the gate] I shouted: 'This company is dismissed for two minutes, when it will fall in again on the other side of the gate.'"

As time went by, Lincoln's level of influence with others in the militia actually decreased. While other officers proved themselves and gained rank, Lincoln found himself going in the other direction. He began with the title and position of captain, but that did him little good. He couldn't overcome the Law of Influence. By the end of his military service, Abraham Lincoln found his rightful place, having achieved the rank of private.

Fortunately for Lincoln—and for the fate of our country—he overcame his inability to influence others. He followed his time in the military with undistinguished stints in the Illinois state legislature and the U.S. House of Representatives. But over time and with much effort and personal experience, he became a person of remarkable influence and impact.

Here is my favorite leadership proverb: "He who thinks he leads, but has no followers, is only taking a walk." If you can't influence others, they won't follow you. And if they won't follow, you're not a leader. That's the Law of Influence. No matter what anybody else tells you, remember that leadership is influence—nothing more, nothing less. **C**

John C. Maxwell speaks to hundreds of thousands of people each year. He is the author of more than thirty books, including the best-selling *The 21 Irrefutable Laws of Leadership.* Look for his newest title, *25 Ways to Win with People*, a follow-up to *Winning With People* that highlights twenty-five specific actions for building great people skills. For more information visit **www.injoy.com**.

Be Influential

By VALORIE BURTON

The month I turned 24, I took an entrepreneurial leap of faith. I left my position as marketing director for an accounting firm and created a public relations firm with my former employer as my first client. My firm's job was essentially helping people influence other people. Whether it was a Fortune 500 company looking to influence a particular segment of the population to pay for their services, or a mega-church seeking to influence the media to write a powerful story that might influence more people to walk through their doors on Sunday morning, our PR services all boiled down to influencing people.

My question to you is this: How are your "Personal PR" skills? Do you live and communicate in such a way that you have a consistent and positive influence on those in your environment? Influence is the ability to inspire or sway attitudes and behavior towards a particular direction. Great leaders master the ability to influence others long before an official title of leadership is bestowed upon them. In fact, some never receive an official title, but their legacy of influence is felt long after they leave.

Your ability to influence is essential to your success. Your purpose in life is rooted in your ability to influence others in a positive way using your unique gifts, talents and experiences. Think of people who influence you. What is it about them that caused you to be influenced by them?

As you ponder that question, you'll likely connect with the following ten principles. Consider this a ten-step road map to gaining influence and use it to lead in powerful, positive way. They are ten strategies that work, whether your goal is to influence the people you work with, the people you live with, those you know and those you've yet to meet.

Lead yourself first

The first rule of influence is to test just how much influence you have over yourself. Develop self-discipline and you will develop the character that attracts people to you. They will seek you out for advice and follow your leadership because you exhibit success habits that most people know, but neglect. If a person cannot lead himself, he will always experience ongoing turmoil when attempting to lead anyone else. What is your vision? Are your goals specific? Do you have a plan and a deadline to reach them?

Know the purpose of your influence

Having influence should not be about gaining the power to get what you want when you want it. It's not about you, your ego, or worldly power. It is about being a vessel for God and a steward of his resources. Make it a goal to become influential because you want to impact the world with God's love and His ways. Know how you are uniquely meant to influence others. When people cross your path, how will their lives be different because they were influenced by you?

Get out of your way

Don't allow age to limit your success. Be willing to learn and grow continually, but refuse to put yourself in a box that says you won't have significant influence at this stage of your life. You have opportunities to influence every day. Be willing to take risks, take on tasks that will stretch you beyond your comfort zone and empower you to move to the next level more quickly. How are you limiting yourself right now?

Admit your mistakes

Once of the quickest ways to lose influence – and respect – is to see a problem and pretend nothing is wrong. When you make a bad decision or do something you wish you had not done, admit it. Then look for ways to improve. Even ask for help from the very people you wish to influence. By telling the truth, you allow those around you to see that they can trust you, and that you don't pretend to be perfect. Just as importantly, you show them that you respect them and value honesty. A willingness to admit a mistake builds loyalty – and loyalty is a hallmark of influence. What mistakes do you need to own up to right now?

Raise the bar

People are influenced by those they see as ahead of them. If your standards match the masses, your influence is diminished. Be willing to be different and raise the bar so that your standards far exceed common expectations. Raising your standards elevates the vantage point from which you view the world, thereby enlarging your perspective. It is this enlarged perspective that empowers you to see a bigger picture and paint a larger vision. How could you raise the bar at this stage of your life?

Make people feel significant

People want to feel important. It is a basic human need. No one likes to feel insignificant. God Himself declares that each of us is a child of His, loved by Him, and therefore, significant in His eyes. If you – by your words, actions or attitude – cause people to feel significant and empowered, you will increase your influence with them. Many people who hold leadership titles like to feel significant by making others insignificant. They may get their way through force, but they will not enjoy the loyalty and long-term changes that are marked by a leader who leads by influence. Who can you make feel significant today?

Refine your gifts

Your power as a leader lies in the divine gifts and talents that are unique to you. When you use your gifts to serve others, you are living on purpose. You will never find greater success on any other path than the one God meant for you – using the abilities He bestowed upon you. To maximize your influence as a leader, you not only must use your gifts and talents, you must improve them continually. When something comes naturally, it can be easy to rest on your laurels. Make a decision to better by honing your gifts and talents through education, mentorship and practice. In what way are you resting on your laurels?

Accept and use constructive criticism

When you try hard and do your best, it can sometimes be difficult to hear criticism on your performance. Make a decision today to stop taking criticism personally. Even when someone delivers criticism in a not-so-sensitive way, listen. Ask yourself, "Is there any truth to what this person is saying?" If you cannot answer objectively, ask someone else who knows the situation. When you become focused on fully developing your potential, you should want to know your areas of needed improvement. Create a plan of action to use constructive criticism to your advantage by making changes that lead to improvement in the key areas of your life. What criticism are you defensive about? How could you use that criticism to be better?

Speak simply

If you communicate well, you will go far as a leader. In fact, the leaders you observe leaders daily may not be the most talented, but they know how to communicate effectively. They are straightforward and relate well with people. They don't just talk, they listen. When they speak, it is obvious they have spent much time listening to the needs of others because people connect with what they say. Be clear about what you want, speak simply and refuse to beat around the bush. Your influence will be felt when others connect, understand and take action based on the message you communicate. What is your communication style? Are you as good at listening as speaking?

Selectively choose who will influence you

Every true leader must also follow. Be selective about who you allow to influence your decisions, attitude and behaviors. With God as your leading influencer, establish the values that are most important to you – the ones you would like others to embrace as a result of being influenced by you. Then make sure that the influences on your life reflect those same values. If you don't, you subject yourself to being led away from your vision and possibly leading others astray as well. This brings us full circle back to principle #1—Lead yourself first. Who are the key influencers in your life? **C**

Valorie Burton is a sought-after life coach and speaker whose books include *Listen to Your Life*, *What's Really Holding You Back?*, and *Rich Minds, Rich Rewards*. Visit her online at **www.valorieburton.com.**

growth

produce results

stylin' hair

develop leaders

flashy suit

grow people

power tie

THE LEADER'S JOB DESCRIPTION

RECENT SUCCESSES OF TV SHOWS LIKE *THE APPRENTICE* SHARE A COMMON SECULAR VIEW OF WHAT IT TAKES TO BE SUCCESSFUL — *ACHIEVE RESULTS AT ALL COST.* FALLING SHORT IN YOUR PERFORMANCE IS UNACCEPTABLE AND LEADS TO THOSE NOW FAMOUS WORDS, "YOU'RE FIRED!"

BY RICK PACKER

Forget values, put aside integrity, focus only on me and the almightily outcome. Shows like *Survivor*, *The Amazing Race*, and *Fear Factor* all follow a similar theme—produce the desired result now (not tomorrow), in record time, and better than your predecessors. Does this sound similar to your own job? Produce results today, hit the number, increase time to market, and crush the competition.

This is an unforgiving *reality* all of us face in our jobs—with one exception. Reality TV shows have no long-term. There is no need to consider how short-sighted actions impact tomorrow's landscape.

Organizations, on the other hand, need to juggle both the present demand and future expectations. When we focus only on achieving in the moment, we find that today's success is tomorrow's failure. That is why it is critical to have a holistic perspective to our jobs.

YOUR JOB - MY JOB - THEIR JOB

We are all different—from the houses we live in to the cars we drive, to the schools we attend, to our outlook on life. However, regardless of our job description, industry, title or position, our jobs exist for the same reasons. In fact, I believe there are three reasons why any job exists.

REASON NUMBER ONE: PRODUCE RESULTS

Your organization hired you to achieve a desired result. Simply put, they have a need--and your skills, attitude, and credentials help them achieve that need.

Most people spend their entire career focusing on results, and for a good reason. Producing results is rewarded and recognized, important and relevant. However,

we can get caught up in the mindset that producing results is the *whole* part of our job, and sacrifice endless hours on work. In reality, producing results is just *a part* of our job.

The simple truth is that *anyone can produce results.* In his book, *"Choosing to Cheat,"* Andy Stanley suggests there are 1000 people who can do your job as good as if not better than you. This is a relatively bold statement.

Most of you are thinking one of two things right now:
(1) *"If producing results is so easy why am I surrounded by people at work who have not produced anything in years?"*
(2) *"Why such a downward slant on producing results? After all, that is why I go to work."*

Unfortunately, there are a number of people surrounding us at work who are not working out. Bob Orben has been know to say, "There are 7 million Americans not working—and even more if you count those with jobs." Producing results may be the first reason why our jobs exist, but it does not mean everyone achieves this reason.

The second question really deals at the heart of matter. We have all chased the big deal or crammed to meet the deadline. Have you ever heard someone say, "I was created to do this job."? We want to believe that what we do vocationally is unique, special, and makes a difference. It can be—but when you produce a result (whatever that result is), keep it in perspective. Celebrate and enjoy the moment, but recognize it is only the first reason. The other two reasons why your job exists ironically make the first reason much easier to achieve and even more fulfilling.

REASON TWO: GROW PEOPLE

As yesterday's results disappear in the rear view mirror, tomorrow's expectations are on the horizon. Tomorrow you will be asked to do more with less and perform quicker and better. And you *should* be asked to do more as advance your organization's vision. Achieving the vision requires sacrifice, progress, growth, higher numbers, increased shareholder value, better quality, and a consistent approach to exceeding customer expectations. This is a business cycle that defines our post-modern expectations of organizations. This cycle will be waiting for you and me tomorrow, and the next day, and the next.

Sounds exhausting, right? People who understand the second reason why their job exists avoid the trap of endlessly worrying about this cycle. They have figured out how to grow the skills sets of the people around them to meet and anticipate tomorrow's demands. Relying on the team's current level of knowledge and skill is not enough to be successful tomorrow. So they spend the time, energy, and effort not only to produce results, but simultaneously grow people.

Growing people is a short-term choice and a long-term commitment. It's much easier to focus on short-term, results oriented success; however, when growing people's skill sets becomes a habit, organizations experience long-term success.

ACTION STEP:
KNOW PEOPLE TO GROW PEOPLE

The first step in growing people is knowing people. Best-selling author John Maxwell has said for years that you need to touch a heart before asking for a hand. In other words, get to know your co-workers before you start asking for their help.

When you ask people what is important to them, and have a genuine desire to hear their response, you build a connection that grants you the permission to start the "growth process." In a formal or informal setting, spend time asking basic questions like, "Where did you grow up?" Then, slowly work to more thought provoking questions such as, "What are you most proud of?" or, "If you could go back in time, what is one thing you would do differently?" This process accelerates trust, which deepens relationships—the building blocks of growing people.

If we don't invest in growing others, our high performing people won't follow us for long. In 2004, Dave Renwick was the caddy for Vijay Singh, the top golfer on the PGA tour. Vijay earned more money in one season than any other professional golfer in history. So why did his caddy quit after that season?

"I just wasn't happy with the ways things were going or the way I was getting treated," Renwick said. "I never got a 'Good morning,' or 'Good club' after a shot, or 'Have a nice night' at the end of the day. It was either nothing or a negative if he did speak to me."

When we do not grow the people around us, the good ones leave and bad ones stay. Both scenarios fail the organization.

REASON THREE: DEVELOP LEADERS

In the life of many leaders, an enormous amount of time is spent organizing meetings, conducting planning processes, and casting vision. They communicate everything in a massive email or through an "all hands meeting." And then, of course they become frustrated two weeks later when the organization has not embraced their masterly crafted strategy. In other words, leaders invest an extreme amount of time leading without the full commitment of those they are leading.

Leaders who find themselves in this scenario have fallen victim to their own success. They are left wondering why the organization is made up of non-committed people who "don't get it." The

"LEADING PEOPLE IN A MANNER THAT THEY WANT TO BE LED, NOT NECESSARILY THEY WAY YOU WANT TO LEAD, AFFORDS YOU THE OPPORTUNITY TO GROW PEOPLE AND ULTIMATELY ACHIEVE RESULTS— RESULTS THAT WILL SUSTAIN BEYOND TODAY."

wondering, however, should be directed back towards their own leadership. Commitment of followers is only gained by seeking out their permission, as opposed to assuming permission is granted.

Why Developing Leaders is Important

So the question that begs to be answered is *Why*? Why is developing leaders the third and most important reason your job exists?

The simplest answer is: growth.

Accomplishing great goals requires great people—people with leadership skills that stretch the organization beyond its current capabilities. Not stretching and then retrenching for a breather, but rather intentionally stretching the organization to accomplish the purpose for which it was designed. And the only way to stretch the organization is through the development of current leaders and the identification and development of new leaders.

Organizations will never admit they have too many leaders. There is no such luxury in today's organizations. In fact, all of us feel the brunt of too little leadership.

ACTION STEP: REFLECT AND RESPOND

Reflect through your own leadership experiences and ask yourself:

- *How would I want to be led?*
- *What would take my commitment level to new heights?*
- *I would willingly follow that person, cause, or initiative because …*

Now switch your focus to those you currently lead and ask yourself:

- *Who in the organization/department has the most potential to lead through tomorrow's challenges?*
- *In what areas can I start developing them now?*

THE POWER OF THREE

When we embrace this holistic perspective regarding our job and why it exists, our work environment improves. Morale is positively impacted. Turnover moves to healthy levels. And most importantly, long-term results reach new heights.

Ask yourself one final question, "Who would you want to work for?" Someone who focuses strictly on producing results? Or, someone who embraces all three reasons why their job (and your job) exists? Leading people in a manner that they want to be led, not necessarily they way you want to lead, affords you the opportunity to grow people and ultimately achieve results—results that will sustain beyond today. **C**

Rick Packer is the President of The Packer Group, an organization that focuses on growing people, improving team cohesiveness, and developing leaders. For more information, or to sign up for Rick's free newsletter, visit **www.thepackergroup.com**.

Journal

What does AUTHENTIC IN INFLUENCE mean to me?

THINK

UNCOMPROMISING in Integrity

How do I make decisions about how I live my life?

Character, conviction, discipline, and decision-making—these all make-up the inner qualities and integrity of a Catalyst leader. I understand that my character and integrity is the guard to my soul and ultimately my life. This can't be let go or delegated. It's the foundation of who I am as a person and as a leader. It's the basis from which my moral authority is grounded. It must be nurtured, guarded and found true under testing.

BY BEN ORTLIP

CALCULATING YOUR INTEGRITY QUOTIENT:
THE ORIGINAL IQ TEST

+ IF YOU THINK BEING SMART CAN SAVE YOU, YOU'RE AN IDIOT

FOR COLLEGE, IT'S YOUR SAT SCORE. FOR A MORTGAGE, IT'S YOUR CREDIT SCORE. AND FOR LIFE IN GENERAL, IT'S YOUR INTEGRITY SCORE. THAT'S RIGHT, JUST WHEN YOU THOUGHT YOU'D BEEN SIZED UP EVERY WAY POSSIBLE, THERE'S YET ANOTHER FACTOR THAT CAN EITHER QUALIFY YOU OR ELIMINATE YOU FROM YOUR MOST TREASURED OPPORTUNITIES IN LIFE. IF YOU DON'T BELIEVE ME, JUST ASK PETE ROSE, MICHAEL JACKSON, OR ANYONE WITH THE WORD "ENRON" ON HIS RESUME.

In fact, your Integrity Quotient is just as likely to influence the quality and direction of your life as your Intelligence Quotient. And the decision-makers of the world know it, too. The suggestion that "character is the issue" was mere fodder for the late-show monologues during the 1990 presidential campaign. And of course, entertainers and other public figures routinely have their integrity gaps showcased in the media, only to emerge with their overall popularity intact. But to those in the trenches of leadership, good old-fashion character is still very much in vogue.

Today, the roster of ethics organizations in America outnumbers tabloid scandal stories three to one. For starters, there's the Institute for Global Ethics. And in case that doesn't cover everything, there are zillions of specialty ethics groups to monitor business, medicine, politics, the media, animal research, and neighborhood bunko. And to keep all those groups ethical, there's even a Council of Ethics-Based Organizations. This is strong evidence that the leaders responsible for year-end profits and organizational progress are serious about integrity. Needless to say, in a budget-driven world, they don't allocate resources for issues like this unless there are measurable financial implications somewhere down the line. Which means it's not just a theory – breaches of integrity can set an organization back ten years and cost millions in damages and lost revenue.

In fact, the science of ethics is emerging as a crucial index in designing success formulas for individuals and institutions. For example, a University of South Carolina study was conducted to measure the impact of character education on behavior and academic performance. The con-clusions showed that 90% of the schools that implemented a character education program reported measurable gains in academic performance, student behavior, and student attitudes. Not surprisingly, 65% also reported improved morale among teachers and staff.

A person's Integrity Quotient is as tangible a predictor of outcomes as any other standardized profiling technique. Moreover, it has the potential to override traditional benchmarks like academic achievement, skills tests, and personality profiles. One chink in the armor of a person's integrity can demote the greatest prodigy to the ranks of the mediocre. And oftentimes, the people around him get sucked down in the undertow. Conversely, someone with average breeding and a high Integrity Quotient will often rise to greatness.

Oddly enough, this drama is played out most conspicuously in the arena of professional sports. These days, it's not enough just to run like a Corvette, jump like a bottle rocket, or throw like an M-16. The men and women who make it in sports today must approach their entire package like a personal brand and manage it accordingly. The ones who understand this seem to settle into long, lucrative careers. The rest usually cause more embarrassment for themselves and their teams than any of their on-field accomplishments can make up for. Sports agents and general managers now know to avoid these prodigal troublemakers before they become a drain on the organization.

But you don't have to be in the business of integrity to know the impact of strong character. Every time you interact with someone, your personal "integrom-

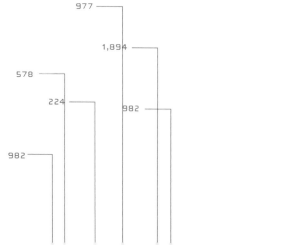

eter" is quietly probing the situation for evidence of personal convictions. You probably don't think about it. But in your subconscious, you notice a pair of eyes that darts away in hopes of avoiding the truth. You recognize the tone of someone putting a spin on a story for the sake of subtle deception. And you can also tell when someone throws personal cost to the wind just because it's the right thing to do.

And it works both ways. People are silently taking notes about you too. Because deep inside, we all know that regardless of how rich or talented or attractive a person may be, integrity can turn into a snake that bites with fierce venom. We've all been betrayed, violated, or otherwise deceived. We know too well the price of leaving ourselves vulnerable to a breach of ethics, whether in the workplace or a neighborhood bunko game. And over the course of a lifetime, we learn how to watch for signs to protect ourselves. The sports teams are protecting themselves. The fans are protecting themselves. And your friends and coworkers are protecting themselves too.

As a result, each of us walks around with a cumulative rap sheet based on our reputation for faithfulness. This aura precedes us wherever we go and it lingers whenever we leave. Like an invisible gatekeeper, it either betrays us or promotes us with the people around us. Your Integrity Quotient is a constant filter between you and the world, either enhancing or tainting people's perceptions about who you are and what you do.

The arena of church leadership is not immune to this principle. In fact, it magnifies it. Nowhere else is your Integrity Quotient so much of a leverage point —

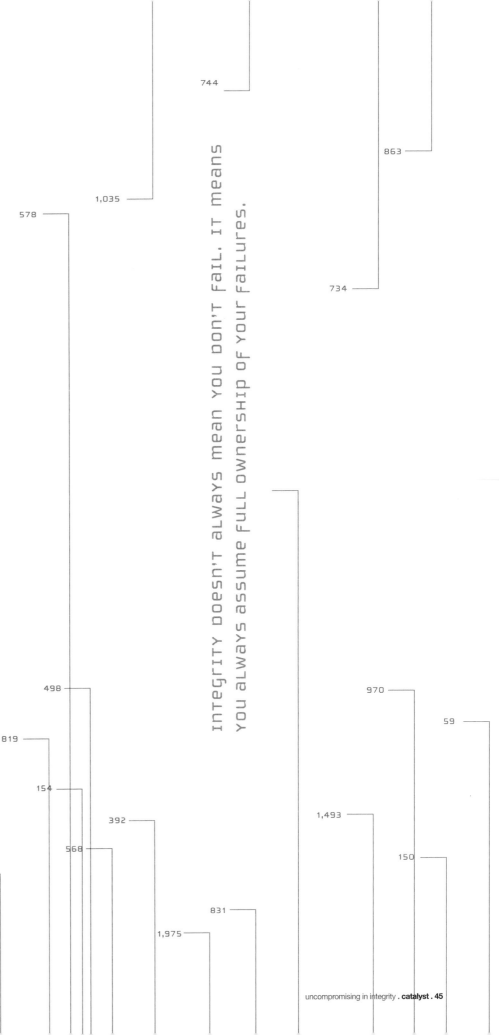

INTEGRITY DOESN'T ALWAYS MEAN YOU DON'T FAIL. IT MEANS YOU ALWAYS ASSUME FULL OWNERSHIP OF YOUR FAILURES.

for better or for worse – than in Christian work. After all, if the professionals can't get it right, it's disingenuous to suggest that the lay people should give it a go.

So have you ever stopped to think about the vibe you're giving off? Of course, you and I both think very highly of you. But we also think you sound just like Coldplay when you sing in the shower. And in case you haven't noticed, the record companies aren't exactly beating down the shower door. Perhaps we could benefit by bringing some objectivity to this assessment. After all, you owe it to yourself to become cognizant of what is probably the greatest variable factor in your life.

Long before the first meeting of Mensa, God had prioritized all the qualities required for success in life. At the top of the list? You guessed it – integrity. At his spiritual coronation, God advised Solomon to, "walk before me in integrity". (1 Kings 9:4 NIV). Nehemiah chose Hanani to be in charge of Jerusalem for the sole reason that, "he was a man of integrity". (Nehemiah 7:2 NIV) The writer of Proverbs included vital observations like, "The man of integrity walks securely," (Proverbs 10:9 NIV) and, "The integrity of the upright guides them" (Proverbs 11: 3 NIV). And as 1 Chronicles 29:17 (NIV) points out, when God tests the heart He is, "pleased with integrity." (NIV) For the record, this constitutes the first IQ test in recorded history.

So how can you quantify your Integrity Quotient? Granted, it's more art than science. But you don't have to be a figure skating judge to come up with a respectable number for it. All you have to do is make a few basic observations about yourself. Here are four factors to consider:

1) DO YOU AVOID CERTAIN PEOPLE?

As you think back over your life, are there any people you hope you never have to face again? On the surface, this is simply a sign of an unpleasant experience. And many of these unpleasant experiences were probably not your fault. But some of your uncomfortable memories could be lingering reminders of a moment or a season in life when your treatment of others (or yourself) didn't live up to your current convictions.

Such an experience represents a deduction in your Integrity Quotient. These offenses take place at a spiritual level and cannot be erased except through spiritual responsibility. Moving away won't help, and neither will growing older. The Bible describes steps of forgiveness and restitution for various offenses. And until you've followed through, you may always feel a little uncomfortable with certain people from your past.

Now, we're not saying you should never forgive yourself. But if you've never taken responsibility for your actions, the Giver of peace may withhold peace in order to call it to your attention. Integrity doesn't always mean you don't fail. It means you always assume full ownership of your failures.

Is there any unfinished business from your past that keeps you from having a clear conscience about your present or your future? It's never too late to go back and take care of it. Even if you've lost contact with the other party (darn the luck), you can still get right with God on the matter. Is there any restitution that needs to be made? Are there any trusted friends who can help you navigate the situation – someone who isn't afraid to challenge you to face what might be uncomfortable? Remember, it doesn't have to feel right to be the right thing to do. And once you've done all you can about it, move on.

2) DO YOU STRUGGLE WITH INSECURITY?

Self-esteem is another factor to consider when calculating your Integrity Quotient. If you struggle to feel good about yourself, it could be an indication of secret sins. Numbers 32:23 says, "Be sure your sin will find you out."(NIV) And even when the rest of the world hasn't found out about our sin yet, we still know. Sometimes that's worse than if we just went on Jerry Springer to tell the whole world and got it over with. We always wonder, "What if they knew the truth about me?"

Secret sin, even though undiscovered, is an integrity issue. And while the world around you may never know what's going on inside, there's a good chance they'll get enough of a creepy feeling to lose confidence about your character. This too is a deduction in your Integrity Quotient.

At the other end of the spectrum, a person in right standing with God is more likely to feel confident and secure. He can look a stranger in the eye without fear of what that person might think about him. Psalm 118:6 says, "The Lord is with me; I will not be afraid. What can man do to me?" (NIV) Notice that you can either feel good about yourself because you live above reproach or because you have forgiveness in Christ.

The best way to rid yourself of insecurity caused by sin is to follow the advice of James 5:16 and find someone you trust to confess it. Don't be surprised if you tell your ugly story and get an unexpected response like, "Hey, I did that too!" When you finally discover that you are perfectly acceptable in the body of Christ despite your past failures, your self-esteem will skyrocket.

3) WHAT DO PEOPLE SAY ABOUT YOU?

In a world of perfect Christians, we'd always know where we stood. Because if anyone had a beef with us, we'd be the first to hear about it. (Matthew 18:15 NIV) Unfortunately, we can't always rely on the people around us to let us know when there's moral spinach in our teeth — probably because they're too busy checking their own. Nevertheless, they can still be the best sources for objectivity and insight when it comes to integrity.

Let's be clear. You shouldn't live your life as a man-pleaser, tossed about by every little opinion about you. However, if you think you can handle the truth, a trusted friend can be mighty helpful when it comes to discovering your blind spots. All you have to do is ask.

More specifically, here's how to do it. First, tell the person why you want to know. This will help him understand just how honest to be. Tell him you have been thinking about integrity and are collecting input for a personal integrity checkup. Tell him you need honesty, no matter how uncomfortable it may be. Next, ask the person to rate your integrity on a scale of one to 10. In addition, ask him how he thinks other people would rate you. Finally, ask him to share any specific high or low points on your integrity rap sheet that impacted your score. You may also ask him what he thinks you should do about it.

Have this conversation with two or three men or women of God and you should start to see a consistent theme emerge. If you approach it humbly, and pray for wisdom, God will make His will known to you.

4) WHAT DO YOU SAY ABOUT PEOPLE?

Sometimes the best measure of your Integrity Quotient comes right out of your own mouth. The higher your integrity, the less likely you are to be critical of others. In contrast, if you have a cynical or critical streak, it could be an indication that you're trying to mask a shortcoming of your own. It's a principle that the one who strikes an offense is often indefensible. In other words, many of our critical remarks are nothing more than a preemptive attempt to compensate for our own inadequacies. When you know deep inside that you don't measure up, it's tempting to bring others down to create a relative equilibrium for yourself. And if anyone's aware of your integrity gaps, it's you.

Of course, this doesn't mean every off-color remark is a sign that someone is hiding a felony record. But everyone can benefit from a long, hard look in the mirror once in a while. In light of your shortcomings, do you wish to call attention to someone else's malfunctions? Or are you driven by a desire to see you both improve? When you truly embrace the reality of your own sinfulness – and God's forgiveness – it's nearly impossible to take issue with another person's sin.

Set aside a day or two to become a student of your own speech. Try to notice what comes out of your mouth. Is it edifying to all? Or opportunistic for some? Either way, it will affect your Integrity Quotient.

INTERPRETING YOUR IQ SCORE

Whether you measure it on a scale of one to 100, or A through F, these four factors should help you get a general feel for the moral vibe you give off. If nothing else, it should make you aware of the significance of some of the little decisions we make each day. Your Integrity Quotient is one of the highest leverage points in your life. Of all the things you can alter about yourself, nothing holds more potential for life change than this.

Granted, there are no quick fixes. If your track record hasn't been perfect, it can take some time for your batting average to climb. But don't forget, when God is honored, He extends honor. And while there aren't any short cuts for establishing a reputation of enduring faithfulness, God will give you the favor you need to accomplish His will for the rest of your life. Even the king's heart is in His hands, to elevate your reputation with him as necessary (Proverbs 21:1 NIV). When your Integrity Quotient is heading in the right direction, you look a little smarter to everyone. **C**

Ben Ortlip writes books and study curriculum for several prominent Christian authors and oversees creative projects for trend-setting ministries like Campus Crusade for Christ, Injoy, FamilyLife, Walk Thru the Bible, and North Point Ministries. Ben is the co-author of the breakout small group study *Blueprint For Life*. He and his wife, Lisa, live in Cumming, Georgia with their six children.

498

982

1,894

867

150

FOR GROUP DISCUSSION:

use these questions and journal pages to reflect and respond to what you've just read.

1 — *In what ways is your reputation important to your future opportunities?*

2 — *How has your reputation helped or hindered your life so far? Give examples.*

3 — — *Based on what you've read, how would you rate your Integrity Quotient? Explain.*

4 — — *What specific events or situations in your life have had the greatest impact?*

5 — — *What action(s) do you need to take as a result of this study?*

DEEP DIVE
Download a complete smallgroup leader's guide at **www.catalystgroupzine.com**

For more on what God has to say about living a life of integrity and character, check out Numbers 32:23; 1 Chronicles 29:17; 1 Kings 9:4-5; Proverbs 10:9, 11:3, 21:1; Matthew 18:15-18; and James 5:16.

THE
DIAMOND LIFE

BY KEVIN MYERS

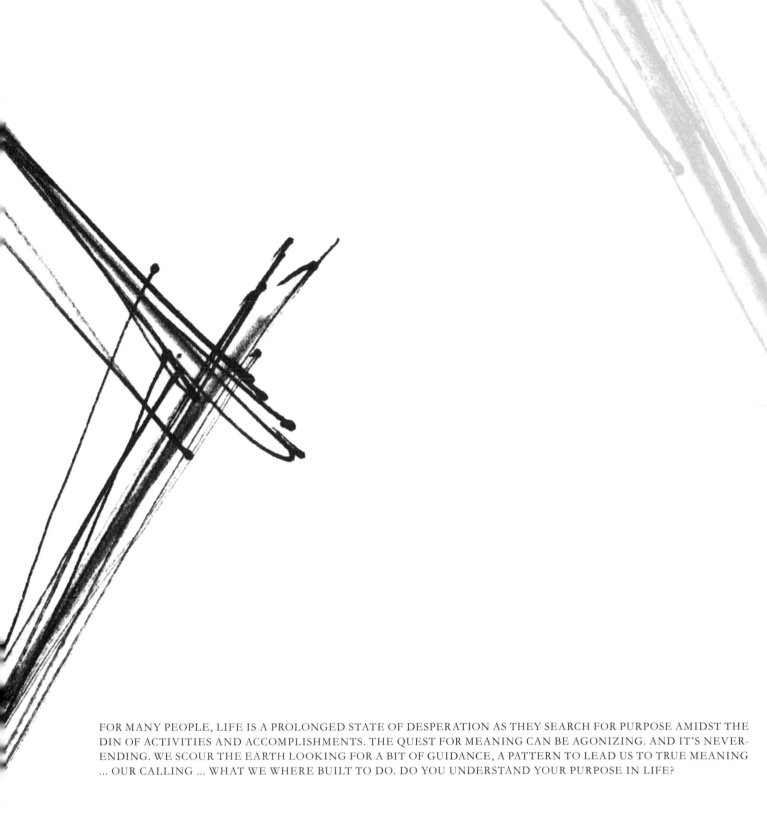

FOR MANY PEOPLE, LIFE IS A PROLONGED STATE OF DESPERATION AS THEY SEARCH FOR PURPOSE AMIDST THE DIN OF ACTIVITIES AND ACCOMPLISHMENTS. THE QUEST FOR MEANING CAN BE AGONIZING. AND IT'S NEVER-ENDING. WE SCOUR THE EARTH LOOKING FOR A BIT OF GUIDANCE, A PATTERN TO LEAD US TO TRUE MEANING ... OUR CALLING ... WHAT WE WHERE BUILT TO DO. DO YOU UNDERSTAND YOUR PURPOSE IN LIFE?

Thankfully, God has answered the enduring question of purpose for us already. He has given us an earthly and eternal purpose that serves as both our launching and landing pad in life.

In Romans 12:1-2, Paul begs the Romans to offer their lives "as a living sacrifice" to God. He goes on to say, "Do not change yourselves to be like the people of this world." In these verses we discover an important pattern for life. We're not to change ourselves to be like the world. But change does need to happen. In fact, the Spirit of God wants to bring about change in the world by first changing us from within.

There is a metaphor that can help us wrap our minds around this concept. Think of it like the bases in a baseball diamond. You begin at home plate. You finish at home plate. And you must cover all the bases—in the right order. This is how the Diamond Life works.

HOME PLATE: THE PURPOSE BASE

The basic diamond begins at home plate with your purpose—what you were created to do. Knowing your purpose involves winning dependency. You must first understand that God has put you here for a purpose—to abide in Him. You gain confidence in your purpose by remaining totally dependent on Him.

In the story of Joseph, son of Jacob, winning dependency on God was no small task. In the beginning of his journey, Joseph was sold into slavery by his jealous brothers. They stripped him of his coat of many colors, his home, his family, his influence and his position as favorite son. Joseph had everything that he had grown to depend on stripped from him until he was left without anything of himself. This is when God was cultivating a dependency upon Him in Joseph's heart that came to define Joseph's leadership for the rest of his life.

Only with true surrendered dependency can we live under the favor that God intends for us. There is usually a period of brokenness initiated by the Holy Spirit that is basic to bearing fruit that lasts. It spawns the growth from self-reliance to Spirit-reliance.

It is important that we begin at this base, with this principle. Just as God crafted in Joseph's life the clarity to start and finish with God on home plate, so must we live in humble, unrelenting dependency.

FIRST BASE: WIN WITHIN

The very first thing that the power of God is designed to do in your life is change you. His highest goal is not to change performance. The Spirit of God is in the business of internal restoration.

Joseph had to learn to win within. During Joseph's journey he is placed as a slave in the house of Potiphar where he is gaining leadership. He is soon tested in his leadership when he is tempted by Potiphar's wife to engage in sexual indiscretion. This was not a small test. Joseph was being tested internally. This test would determine whether or not he could trust himself. Joseph resisted giving honor and respect to Potiphar, to God, and to himself. Self-leadership always precedes leading others.

The first base is all about character and God's desire to reshape us in His image. The fourth chapter of James tells us why there are quarrels and breakdowns among believers. It is because of the war within all of us. We have unresolved desires, immature emotions, unknown motives, and deep self-deception. We must get honest with God about character issues.

SECOND BASE: WIN WITH OTHERS

As you win within the personal base, you gain credibility to go to second base and win with others in community. It is only within a team where you can experience what God can leverage through your leadership gift in the lives of others.

Joseph had to learn to win with others. Early in his life, Joseph was very comfortable being favored by his father. There must have been deep-seeded hurt in his brothers to willingly cast their brother aside and claim he was dead, but Joseph was not sensitive to the pain of his brothers.

Later in his life, Joseph was sold as a slave and treated without distinction. Stripped from his father's favor, Joseph discovered the sorrow and struggles of others. Nothing compares to being on the same level with people to realize how to treat others with dignity—to serve them and care for them and cease being self-absorbed. No one wants to hear a vision in which you are standing and they are bowing.

Only authentic dependency on God will free us from deep-rooted, self-serving motives. God will give you the power to deal with the truth of the issues within that prevent you from winning with others.

THIRD BASE: WIN OVER OBSTACLES

This is the performance base. Third base is all about success—success in our careers, in our families, in everything we do. Third base, however, is not the end. You do not score on third base because success that lasts ultimately brings about the eternal purposes that God has intended in your life.

Have you ever watched the very first game of the season in a tee-ball league? Let me help you envision it. Little kids wearing baseball hats two sizes too big take turns getting up to bat. The objective is clear: hit the ball off the tee and run around the bases. Batter up. Johnny, with explosive excitement, hits the ball off the tee. He stands stunned at home plate while parents and coaches shout, "Run, Johnny! Run!" Dozens of little feet all scamper to get the ball. Johnny's little heart pounds as he begins to run, but Johnny does not quite understand the great game of baseball yet. He runs straight for 3rd base and high-tails it for home plate. Johnny hit a homerun—at least in his book.

The pattern of the world tells us to run to third base first. We are a performance-driven society that finds value in what we do and the results we generate. We were built for work, but Satan takes the design of God and flips it around to confuse us. When we run the bases backward, though, there is immense pressure to cheat home plate, cheat integrity and cheat relationships.

God allowed Joseph to experience success in Potiphar's house. Then, he was cast into prison as a result of being obedient to God. Yet, God gave Joseph favor and allowed him success again through interpreting dreams. Joseph, however, thought Potiphar's dream was all about Joseph's rise, but God was at work in a much greater way. Ultimately Joseph saved a nation. God's vision is always bigger than ours.

BACK HOME

If we fix our hearts on finishing well, our lives will bring us right back to the place of purpose at which we started. Every step of the journey—from base to base—comes back to this foundation. Completing the process requires that we never lose sight of that goal. We must not think that our ultimate destination is any of the other bases. We must yearn to press on until God has His way with us completely. As Christians mature, it can be tempting to invent new missions to accomplish. But in this game, the idea is to start on-purpose and to finish on-purpose. Sometimes, the final stretch can be the most difficult to master. Only when our purpose is clear can we enjoy the sense of focus that comes from serving God. And that's when we can cross the plate with the satisfaction that our job is "well done."

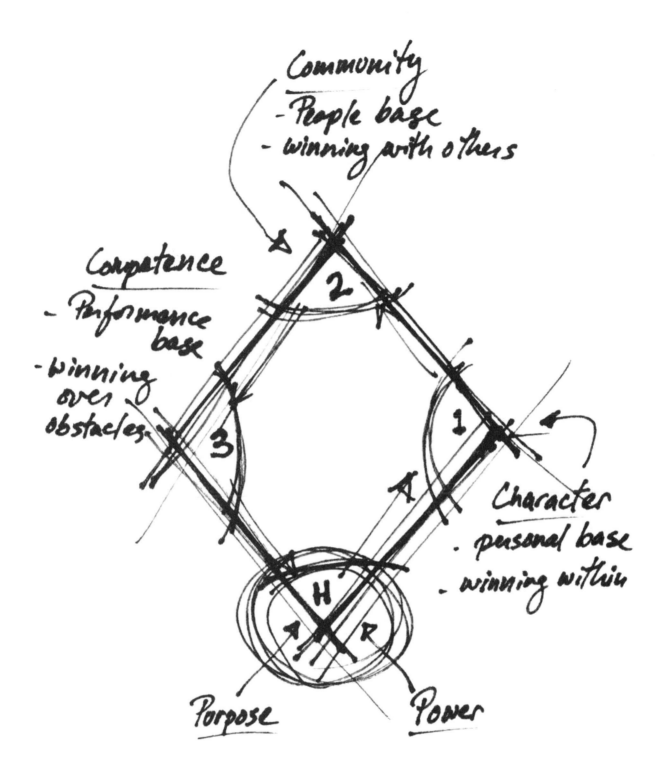

Community
- People base
- winning with others

Competence
- Performance base
- winning over obstacles

Character
- personal base
- winning within

Purpose

Power

PLAY BY THE RULES

God's pattern cultivates the personal and relational authenticity we long to experience. Everyday, I wake up knowing I am dependent on God, but I instinctively run to third base. I resort to my tee-ball logic that says all I need to do is figure out some way to make it to home base. But God has a distinctive plan in which the order of the bases matter, and He will grant us favor with each challenge along the way, one base at a time. **C**

Kevin Myers is the Senior Pastor of the rapidly growing Crossroads Community Church in Lawrenceville (metro Atlanta), Georgia (**www.crossroads connect.com**). Look for Kevin's first book to be published in the near future. Register for updates at **www.kevinmyers.org**. Kevin and his wife, Marcia, have been married for 23 years and have four children.

TRUE STORY

Creating a New Existence

JOSH HOTSENPILLER

Josh Hotsenpiller could have chosen an easy path. Having been raised in a successful pastor's home on the East Coast, he knew the ins and outs of church ministry, and had connections through his family's mega church that would have given him an easy ride in ministry. Josh was gifted in many areas, described as flamboyant, charismatic, and a natural leader.

But Josh chose instead to leave his comfort zone and drive across country to San Diego, California, putting down roots there with only his wife and a handful of friends who followed him. He believed God was calling him to plant a church, and so he set out to do just that.

But old habits and beliefs die hard. "The reality was," Josh said, "that we had moved out here to start a church that people would flock to and call the greatest church around." He learned quickly that God had a different plan—a plan to change Josh's heart and break his pride.

"For years I was taught that our identity is found in what we accomplish, and for me, my accomplishments were small," he reflects. God used the next 12 months at Josh's church plant, called Existence Church, to begin to expose Josh to the truth of His love and God's value system. "True value in God's eyes is found in daily living out our calling from Him," Josh says. "For so long, I was attempting to live out the calling given from ME, and each day feeling more empty."

So while attendance was low and conversions were few, the first year of existence for Existence Church provided a soil rich in lessons of God's love, grace, and acceptance that not only Josh needed to learn, but his small flock as well. Their ministry began to take on a servant focus, with Josh leading through servant hood. Six months ago they watched as God began to transform lives. Many have received Jesus as Savior and are getting grounded in the love and acceptance of Jesus Christ.

Existence Church (**www.existencechurch.com**) has moved from a rented school gym to a fully furnished warehouse perfectly suited for their needs—all because of the generosity of God's people who are seeing Him work in mighty ways.

Josh is still the persuasive, gifted communicator that friends and family "back home" knew, and yet he's changed in so many ways. "Our final hope is to wait with great expectations on God," Josh says. "We believe as He grows and matures us, we will naturally make greater impacts for His Kingdom!" C

TRUE STORY

NAEEM FAZAL

Held Hostage by His Love

Naeem Fazal, to many who know him in Charleston, South Carolina, doesn't seem the type who once threatened his brother with death if he shared the gospel with their parents. But it's true.

Naeem's path to faith in Jesus Christ began in 1989 when his brother returned home to Kuwait and announced that he had given his life to the Lord while in the United States. Upon hearing the news, Naeem threatened to kill him if he shared this "good news" with their parents. After all, he said, "We were a Pakistani Muslim family of seven—three brothers and two sisters born in the Middle East."

In 1992, Naeem came to Charleston to study art, and began attending meetings of the Fellowship of Christian Athletes (FCA). It was at one particular meeting that Naeem challenged God to prove Himself. Three nights later, he was convinced that God was who He said He was, and he accepted Christ as his personal Savior.

Soon after his conversion, Naeem sensed a call from God to pursue a job in ministry. He directed the junior high ministry at Seacoast Church in Charleston, and later became involved in leadership in other areas as well, such as the young adults ministry that spun off a number of successful video campus ministries.

Naeem, gifted in communication skills, says, "The gospel is a lot more simple when you don't have to convince men and women to accept Christ, but rather challenge them to ask God to show Himself." Struck by the love of God, Naeem believes, "Serving God has got to come from a heart grateful that God loves me so much." He says, "That kind of love should propel us to do what God calls us to do. That's the fuel that will never go empty. God has held me hostage by love."

He recognizes the importance of being honest with himself and God. "I've got to look in the mirror and say, 'This is who I am.' It would be a lack of integrity," Naeem believes, "if I pursue anything else that I shouldn't be."

His family no doubt has seen the integrity and character of Naeem's life, as he reflects Jesus Christ to them. Over the years, Naeem has had the privilege of leading his two brothers and two sisters to Christ, while still praying and expecting Mom and Dad to join them one day.

Naeem will soon be launching a new church in Charlotte, North Carolina called Mosaic Church. (**www.mosaicchurch.tv**) **C**

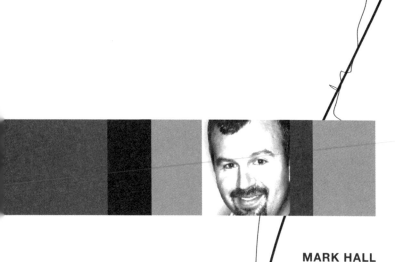

TRUE STORY

An Authentic Artist

MARK HALL

Mark Hall is the lead singer of Casting Crowns, winner of seven Dove Awards, whose album has recently reached the platinum mark, only sixteen months after its debut. Last year Casting Crowns performed to more than 140 audiences stateside and internationally. However, roving the country on a highly successful tour is just a slice of his mission.

Hall's mainstay calling is not in the world of Christian music—it's ministering to youth within his church, Eagles Landing Baptist Church in McDonough, Georgia. (**www.eagleslanding.org**) "As a band, we get to travel and plant seeds, but the church is the centerpiece," Mark says. He realizes the benefit of having a life that doesn't revolve around his band. "I need accountability. I need to not be allowed to coast on ten cool songs and stories." Serving as youth pastor, he believes, keeps him "in a situation where I am fresh."

While on the road, Mark believes in authenticity, not only because his family travels with him, but because of what his audience needs to see. "Integrity ... defines what you are all about," he says. "One thing that hits me on the road is that these people don't need another hero or another buddy—they need to know God. So everything I say on stage has to point to Him and not me."

Despite the temptation to make ministry a means to prosperity, Mark continues to follow God's lead and not his own. He realizes that he's only a channel of God's grace, and right now, God is using Mark's musical talent and his passion for youth to reflect God's love. "I've got to remind myself every day," Mark says, "that my purpose is to be like Jesus and not write records." **C**

YOUR STORY

Integrity is hard to define, but easy to identify. Your character and integrity is what makes you a leader worth following. Think about a friend or mentor in your community who lives a life of high integrity. List the character qualities they possess. Now, ask yourself, "Do I demonstrate these qualities?" Write a story of what your leadership and life looks like when you demonstrate character and integrity.

A NON-ESSENTIAL

BY ANDY STANLEY

Let's begin with a reality check: Character is not essential to leadership. We all know of leaders who have led large organizations and garnered the loyalty of many followers, and yet lacked character. They demonstrated courage and competency. They were clear in their directives. They may have even sought the advice of others. But they were not men and women who were known for doing what was right. It is not uncommon to hear accomplished leaders attribute their success to business practices and personal conduct that most people would consider reprehensible. And yet there they are, king or queen of the mountain...at least for the moment.

As we discussed earlier, you can lead without character. But character is what makes you a leader worth following. Integrity is not necessary if your aspirations as a leader end with simply persuading people to follow you. But if at the end of the day your intent is for those who follow to respect you, integrity is a must. Your accomplishments as a leader will make your name known. Your character will determine what people associate with your name.

Your gifts and determination may dictate your potential, *But it is your character that will determine your legacy.* You can create an enviable lifestyle by leveraging your leadership skills alone. But you cannot create an enviable life without giving serious attention to who you are on the inside.

Authors James Kouzes and Barry Posner surveyed nearly 1,500 managers from around the country as part of a study sponsored by the American Management Association. They asked the following open-ended question: "What values, personal traits, or characteristics do you look for and admire in your superiors?" In other words, what makes a leader worth following?

More than 225 values, traits, and characteristics were identified. These were then reduced to fifteen categories. What these managers said they wanted most from their leaders was integrity. The categories that scored the highest marks were "integrity," "is truthful," "is trustworthy," "has character," and "has convictions."(1)

In a subsequent study they elaborated on several categories and added a few new characteristics not included in the previous study. In a two-year series of executive seminars conducted at Santa Clara University and several corporate locations, more than 2,600 top-level managers completed a checklist of superior leadership characteristics. The number-one characteristic they looked for in a leader was honesty. Honesty ranked ahead of "competency," "intelligence," and "is inspiring." (2)

These findings are supported by a study conducted jointly by Korn/Ferry International and Columbia Graduate School of business. Surveying more than 1,500 top executives in twenty countries, the study looked into strategies for growth, areas of expertise, and personal characteristics of the ideal CEO. "Ethics" was rated most highly among the personal characteristics needed by a CEO. In short, they expected their leaders to be above reproach.(3)

Those who choose to follow you want you to be a leader worth following. They will judge you not so much for where you led them, but how you led them. Their stories will always include their personal estimation of you as a person, not just your leadership skills. The truth is that those who choose to follow you will expect more from you by way of character than they expect from themselves.

Years ago I adopted a definition of character that is simple enough for me to remember yet complete enough to have teeth: Character is the will to do what's right even when it's hard.

Character is about *will* because it requires a willingness to make tough decisions—decisions that sometimes run contrary to emotion, intuition, economics, current trends, and in the eyes of some, common sense. Having the will to do what's right requires that you determine what's right before the struggle to do what's right ensues. Leading with character necessitates a series of predecisions. As a next generation leader you must decide ahead of time what is nonnegotiable as it relates to right and wrong.

When we talk about the will to do what's right, we are assuming the existence of a standard of right and wrong that exists apart from us, an unmoving bar by which we are measured. Leaders worth following acknowledge an absolute standard of right and wrong, one that exists independent of their emotions, experiences, or desires. They lead with the assumption that there is a benchmark by which all decisions are judged.

Granted, it is not popular to speak in terms of absolutes. But as C. S. Lewis asserted:

Whenever you find a man who says he doesn't believe in real right or wrong, you will find the same man going back on this a moment later. He may break his promise to you, but if you try breaking one to him he'll be complaining "It's not fair" before you can say Jack Robinson.(4)

Character involves doing what's right because it's the right thing to do—regardless of the cost. And it's those last few words that divide the men and women of character from those with good but negotiable intentions.

The most direct path to where you want to be is not the most ethical one. How do I know that about you? After all, we have never met! I will be the first to admit that it is unfair for me to judge your situation without knowing anything about it. But my hunch is that if you were to draw a straight line from where you are to where you want to be, and then follow it, you would be forced to compromise morally or ethically. Somewhere between you and your goal as a next generation leader there is a minefield.

The day will come when progress seems to call for a compromise of conviction. The leader in you will want to push forward. After all, you've come so far. The end certainly justifies the means. In that moment the significance of the goal will far outweigh the significance of the compromise. But there will be another voice as well. The message will be simple, short, and without explanation: "This is wrong." Against that still, small voice you will hurl one thousand reasons, explanations, rationalizations, and illustrations. But when you are finished, the undaunted voice inside you will continue to whisper, "It's not right."

As you will discover, if you haven't already, the shortest distance between where you are and where you want to be is not the most honorable one.

The good news is that in most cases there are other paths you can take. But they are generally longer, steeper, and more

 YOUR GIFTS AND DETERMINATION MAY DICTATE YOUR POTENTIAL, BUT IT IS YOUR CHARACTER THAT WILL DETERMINE YOUR LEGACY.

expensive. Nobody likes to detour. Especially leaders. But what hangs in the balance of those inevitable dilemmas is worth the delay.

The irony of being a leader with character is that your willingness to do what is right may jeopardize your forward motion. Leading and being the person you want to be don't always line up. But it is in those moments that you discover a great deal about yourself. You discover what you value most.

Predeciding to do what's right will cost you. It will cost you time, money, and opportunity. It may negatively impact your reputation...at least for the short term. It may actually be an obstacle on your career path.

As a next generation leader you may be tempted to believe that once you attain a certain level of success, these kinds of dilemmas will dissipate. If you think this, you are mistaken. Success doesn't make

I have a good friend who took his company public several years ago. Up until that time he was committed to being known in his industry as a man of impeccable integrity. His charismatic personality combined with his unwavering character was infectious. Within a relatively short time he was able to find the venture capital he needed to launch what became something of an overnight success in the print industry. Throughout the process he was careful not to take shortcuts morally or ethically.

But as he made his way up the last incline, with the top of the mountain in sight, something changed. The influx of money brought on by the IPO combined with the pressure of greedy stockholders began to take its toll on him. Fear choked the life out of his vision. His quest for progress seemed to be replaced by an irrational dread of losing what he had acquired. He became defensive. Eventually he began taking medication to ease his anxiety. Throughout this ordeal he was quick to

cessful leaders playing by a different set of rules. Everything really does look different when you are at the top.

Power, money, success, fame...they are all intoxicants. And intoxicated people see the world differently. For the intoxicated leader, rules are for the common man. Not for him. What was once unthinkable becomes necessary in light of what's at stake. What was once considered dishonest is seen as prudent in light of current reality. When questioned, his response is something along the lines of, "One day you will understand."

Maybe you read a paragraph like that and think to yourself, *Not me. I'll be different.* Perhaps you will be one of the few who is able to carry the weight of success without bending to the pressure that comes with it. Or perhaps when that day arrives, you will consider your current outlook on life naive and you'll find yourself considering options you'd always ruled out. Time will tell.

WE ARE ALWAYS ONE DECISION, ONE WORD, ONE REACTION AWAY FROM DAMAGING WHAT HAS TAKEN YEARS TO DEVELOP.

anything of consequence easier. Success just raises the stakes. Success brings with it the unanticipated pressure of maintaining success. The more successful you are as a leader, the more difficult this becomes. There is far more pressure at the top of an organization than you might imagine.

If you are so fortunate as to gain success in the eyes of the public or within your organization, you will wake up one day to the realization that what was once applauded as exceptional is now expected. It is more exciting to win the world heavyweight championship than it is to defend it. It is more exhilarating to break a standing sales record than it is to try to match it year after year.

It is on the mountaintop that leaders often abandon the convictions and humility that got them there. Once they have "arrived" they are tempted to opt for a maintenance strategy that calls for an entirely different set of tools. Whether it is business, politics, or religion, the pressure to compromise in order to maintain one's success is a constant.

give God credit for his past success. But he began to have a difficult time trusting God to help him maintain the success he'd been given.

On more than one occasion I believe this man has compromised his character for the sake of maintaining his business success. When I have questioned him about it, he just shakes his head and says, "Andy, you don't understand." But his condescending tone betrays him. He is the one who is confused, not me. When I press him for more information, his convoluted explanations confirm my suspicion: I think he knows he is wrong. But this is the path he has chosen for now, a path that will continue to lead him away from the things he once valued most.

———————————

It is not just a leader's fear of losing his spot on the top of the mountain that sets him up for compromise. With success comes a propensity to see oneself as the final authority as it relates to right and wrong. It is not uncommon to find suc-

Either way, the temptation will be there to rewrite the rules.

What if you knew you could break the rules, change the rules, or even ignore the rules and get away with it? What if you knew there would never be any consequences financially or physically? Then what would you do?

Leading with character is not about doing right to avoid consequences. Leaders worth following do the right thing because it is the right thing. Virtue is not a means to an end. It is the end.

Leaders worth following don't make the rules. They lead within the guidelines that have been established before they ever came onto the scene. They recognize and submit to what is right as right has been defined by God in the hearts of men. Leaders worth following acknowledge that their leadership skills and successes never give them the right to replace what God has put in place.

Right and wrong are not determined by economic and organizational progress. They stand apart from both. At times they stand in the way of both. It is not until right and wrong impede forward motion that you discover if you are a leader worth following.

So why cling tenaciously to something that has the potential to slow you down? If leadership for the sake of personal advancement is all you are after, then there is no compelling reason. But if you desire to be a leader worth following, you really have no choice.

Here's why: What hangs in the balance of your decision to choose the way of character verses expedience is something far more valuable to you as a leader than progress. What hangs in the balance is your moral authority.

Every leader wears two badges: one visible, one invisible. The visible badge is your position and title. The invisible badge is your moral authority.

Your position gives you authority within a certain context, i.e., the office. Your moral authority, however, gives you influence in a variety of contexts. Your position will prompt people in your organization to lend you their hands on a temporary basis. But your moral authority will inspire them to lend you their hearts.

Moral authority is established once it becomes clear to those who are watching that progress, financial reward, and recognition are not a leader's gods. When they see that, as much as you value those things, there is something you value more, something you refuse to sacrifice at the altar of "success," you will have moral authority in their eyes.

Moral authority is the credibility you earn by walking your talk. It is the relationship other people see between what you claim to be and what you really are. It is achieved when there is perceived alignment between conviction, action, belief, and behavior. Alignment between belief and behavior makes a leader persuasive.

The invisible badge of moral authority bestows upon the leader something that money can buy, but only temporarily. With moral authority comes influence.

And it is far easier to lead from the vantage point of influence than position alone. You can manage people without moral authority. But you cannot influence them.

We will not allow ourselves to be influenced by men and women who lack moral authority. Inconsistency between what is said and done inflicts a mortal wound on a leader's influence. Consequently, that same inconsistency hampers a leader's ability to lead.

John Maxwell was right when he said that people have to buy into the leader before they will buy into the vision. It is your moral authority that opens the door for the people around you to buy into your vision. You can pay people to work for you based on your position alone, but you cannot involve people in a cause or a movement without moral authority.

Consequently, every decision you make will either add to or detract from the influence you have with those who have chosen to follow you—even those decisions that are not directly related to your profession.

Leaders worth following do not pretend to live in two worlds. There is no discrepancy between their professional and private lives. They know the futility of compartmentalizing their lives.

You can tell yourself all day that how you conduct your life away from the office is nobody's business. Perhaps you are right. But do not be deceived: If there is a perceived difference between what you expect from others and what you expect from yourself, it will eventually erode your influence.

As a pastor who grew up in a pastor's home I know this all too well. Every time I take my family to a restaurant people have an opportunity to see whether or not I really live what I preach. How realistic is it to think that people can see me act one way in public and yet espouse a totally different standard on Sunday morning and maintain their respect for me as a leader? I may successfully compartmentalize my life, but they won't be able to.

Your situation is no different. To be a leader worth following there must be alignment between the values you preach to your organization and the values you live out in every facet of your life. If you require honesty from those you work with, then honesty must be a trait that characterizes you in all your roles.

Your position in the company may be secure, but your influence and moral authority will remain fragile. We are always one decision, one word, one reaction away from damaging what has taken years to develop. **C**

1. *James M. Kouzes and Barry Z. Posner,* The Leadership Challenge *(San Francisco: Jossey-Bass, Inc., 1987), 16.*
2. *Ibid., 17*
3. *James M. Kouzes and Barry Z. Posner,* Credibility *(San Francisco: Jossey-Bass, Inc., 1993), 15.*
4. *C.S. Lewis,* The Case for Christianity *(New York: Macmillan Publishers, 1943), 5.*

Excerpted from The Next Generation Leader © *2003 by Andy Stanley. Used by permission of Multnomah Publishers, Inc.*

Andy Stanley is a graduate of Dallas Theological Seminary and the founding pastor of Northpoint Community Church (**www.northpoint.org**) in Atlanta, with a youthful congregation of more than 12,000. Andy has authored numerous best-sellers including *Visioneering, Like a Rock, The Next Generation Leader,* and the recent *How Good is Good Enough.* Andy and his wife Sandra have two sons and a daughter.

THE ICEBERG

By Tim Elmore

THE ICEBERG REPRESENTS YOUR LEADERSHIP. THE 10% ABOVE THE WATER IS YOUR SKILL. THE 90% BELOW THE WATER IS YOUR CHARACTER. IT'S WHAT'S BELOW THE SURFACE THAT SINKS THE SHIP.

An iceberg is an interesting picture of the first rule of leadership. There's more to it than what meets the eye. Most of an iceberg is below the surface of the water.

You probably remember the awesome story of the Titanic. (Maybe you saw the movie!) The huge and unsinkable ship received five iceberg warnings that fateful night of April 14, 1912, just before it went down. When the sixth message came in during the wee hours of the next morning: "Look out for icebergs," the operator wired back, "Shut up! I'm busy." These were his last words over the wire before it all happened. Exactly thirty minutes later, the great vessel—the one whose captain said even God couldn't sink this ship—was sinking. Hundreds of passengers and crew were drowned.

What was the problem? They forgot the truth of the iceberg. What they saw above the water couldn't have sunk the great ship. Unfortunately—most of an iceberg is below the water line. They underestimated the power of the iceberg, and overestimated their own strength. What an accurate description of so many leaders today.

The iceberg is a great picture of leadership because so much of our influence comes from qualities we can't see on the outside. It's stuff below the surface. I estimate 90% of our leadership is made up from our character. And, our character is the sum total of our:

Self-discipline - The ability to do what's right even if you don't feel like it

Core values - Principles you live by that enable you to take a moral stand

Sense of identity - A realistic self-image based on who you are in Christ

Emotional security - The capacity to be emotionally stable and consistent

Many people make it into the limelight, and neglect their character. Your skill may get you to the top—but it's your character that will keep you there. If you don't have strong character, you will eventually sabotage your leadership. You can only fake it so long.

We learned this in the 1980s when so many Christian televangelists fell morally. We learned it again in the 1990s when many politicians fell morally, including our president. We learned it again during the first decade of the new century when corporations such as Enron, WorldCom and Tyco committed moral crimes and pro athletes were taken to court due to lack of character. Even dozens of Catholic priests were charged with sexual crimes.

My explanation? The iceberg. Weak character may begin with lying and cheating on tests. It eventually takes the form of fraud, sex crimes, robbery and scandal.

While leadership skills are good to have—God doesn't want your skills at the expense of your character and integrity. Lead yourself well before you try leading others.

The bad news about icebergs is that it's what's below the surface that sinks a ship. When we have weak character it will eventually damage our ability to lead. The good news about icebergs is that it's what's below the surface that supports the tip of the iceberg. In the same way, strong character will hold you up strong and long enough to use your skills. **C**

Luke 6:43-45 (NASB)

43) For there is no good tree which produces bad fruit; nor, on the other hand, a bad tree which produces good fruit. 44) For each tree is known by its fruit. For men do not gather figs from thorns, nor do they pick grapes from a briar bush. 45) The good man out of the good treasure of his heart brings forth what is good; and the evil man out of the evil treasure brings forth what is evil; for the mouth speaks from that which fills the heart.

These words, spoken by Jesus, are loaded with meaning. We can be sure of at least one conclusion: Whatever is happening on the outside of our life comes from what's happening on the inside. When we see the fruit, we know what kind of tree it is. The outside is only a reflection of what's on the inside.

God puts "being" before "doing." He prioritizes the inside (our heart), because that will determine what goes on outside (our behavior).

Question: Why is focusing on the "inside" so difficult for us today?

Question: Why do we put so much emphasis on the "outside" of our lives?

HOW DO I RATE?

Take a minute and think about your own character. Do you have strong character? On a scale of one to ten (with ten being the strongest), rate yourself in the following areas:

1. Self discipline (The ability to do what is right even if you don't feel like it)

    1 2 3 4 5 6 7 8 9 10

2. Core Values (The principles you live by that enable you to take a moral stand)

    1 2 3 4 5 6 7 8 9 10

3. Sense of Identity (A healthy, realistic self-image based on who you are in Christ)

    1 2 3 4 5 6 7 8 9 10

4. Emotional Security (Your emotional health that enables you to be stable and consistent)

    1 2 3 4 5 6 7 8 9 10

Question: Why did you give yourself the scores you did?

TRY THIS...

Identify several things you really don't like doing. It may be a chore like sweeping out the garage or some other job around the house. It could be cleaning your dorm room or studying on a daily basis. It may be listening to or interacting with someone who seems unlovable. It may be physical exercise or the discipline of waiting. It could be as simple as eating a vegetable you don't like.

Choose two of these "undesirables" and make them disciplines. Deliberately do what you don't like doing. Practice them daily for one week. Put them on the calendar and ask someone to hold you accountable to do them. (If you do them for two weeks, chances are they will become a habit!)

Afterwards, discuss the results. Did you feel a sense of accomplishment? Did you waver in your commitment? Discuss with someone how daily disciplines pave the way for conquering laziness and indifference. How have you gained personal victory by practicing these disciplines?

Adapted from Habitudes: Images that Form Leadership Habits & Attitudes *by Tim Elmore, copyright 2004, Growing Leaders. Used by permission.*

Tim Elmore is founder and president of Growing Leaders. He is has worked with students for over 25 years and is committed to developing next generation of leaders who love God and know how to influence their world. Tim is the author of several books you can find at **www.GrowingLeaders.com**.

fruit markets

HOW the fruit of the spirit reveals God's character to the world

by elisa morgan

A NURSERY OWNER SETS OUT TO SELL PEACH TREES. SHE CONSIDERS APPROACHES. SHE MIGHT PEDDLE PICTURES OF LEAFY SAPLINGS BOUND IN BURLAP SACKS. SHE MIGHT OPEN A FOUR-COLOR CATALOGUE TO PICTURES OF PEACH TREES IN VARIOUS SEASONS OF THE YEAR, BARE BRANCHED, FLOWERING, FRUITING AND POST-FRUIT. BUT WHAT REALLY SELLS A PEACH TREE IS THE PEACH IT PRODUCES: PUNGENT, DEEP ORANGE, FUZZY SKINNED, DANGLING FROM BRANCHES. YOU CAN SEE IT, SMELL IT, TOUCH IT AND TASTE IT. IT'S THE PEACH THAT SELLS THE PEACH TREE.

God is the master marketer. He "packages" himself in a wrapper of fruit: love, joy, peace, patience, kindness, goodness, gentleness, faithfulness and self-control.

Fruit markets. Fruit sells God to a world hungry for truth, for hope and for life. At first that might seem like a "bad" thing. It's not. Fruit is something we know. We're familiar with these amazing words. God is so much bigger but he meets us in the language, words, and qualities of our longing so that we might know him.

Fruit is the external result of an internal relationship. Our fruit represents our character. It is the dressing that beckons others to know the God we represent. Fruit looks good! It smells good! When we get to know fruit-filled people, we discover that fruit tastes good as well.

Like bright peaches standing out against the green leaves of a tree, the fruit of the Spirit announces to a starving world, "Here is food! Here is life! Come and find a way out of exhaustion and discouragement! Come and meet God!"

Love. Joy. Peace. Patience. Kindness. Goodness. Faithfulness. Gentleness. Self-control.

These are the characteristics that describe Jesus to us from Galatians 5. When we focus on the words – just the words – that compose the classic fruit, we pause. Something stirs inside us. Loving? Yes please! Patient? Absolutely! They're attractive qualities. We want them. We long for them in our days and our nights and in all the moments in between. We want to grow a life that matters in ourselves and in those we work alongside. We want them in us and we want to reproduce them in the lives of those we impact. We yearn for God to use us to market himself to a world hungry for hope.

But desiring these characteristics in our lives isn't just for ourselves. As leaders, we want to grow lives that matter in ourselves so that through us, God might reproduce his character in others. Leadership begins and ends with character. Who we are precedes what we do. If we are fruit-filled people, we will live lives that reproduce fruit.

But how? These qualities seem impossible, unrealistic to grow in our everyday lives, much less the lives of anyone else. We're us. Women. Men. Wives, Husbands, some of us. Moms. Dads. On the run. In the trenches. Under stress.

There are three wrongs we need to get right in order to grow a life that matters and to market this fruit-filled life to those around us.

First, the fruit of the Spirit is not about being nice. It's about being like Jesus. Jesus was always loving, joyful, peaceful, patient, kind, good, faithful, gentle and self-controlled. But these qualities didn't always wear the peeling of "nice" in his interactions. His love was acted out in telling a prostitute to stop sinning and religious leaders to quit making faith harder than God intended it to be. His kindness led him to touch an outcast leper during a day when such an action was strictly prohibited. His peace put him to sleep in a boat with disciples in the middle of a storm out at sea. Such moments don't define "niceness". But they were definitely fruit-filled. It's not about being nice.

The fruit of the Spirit are those God-like qualities that make us look like him. They are his nature exhibited in our personalities. When we plant ourselves in a relationship with Jesus, day in and day out, the result of that relationship is the fruit of his characteristics in us. The fruit of the Spirit is what we look like when we're like Jesus.

Second, the fruit of the Spirit is not up to us to grow. It's up to God. Our genetics determine the results of our physical bodies. We can influence the outcome with our efforts but in the end, what we look like—height, shoe-size, eye color—is up to how we're designed. Similarly, while we have a role in the growing process, spiritual growth is up to God.

God's job is fruit production. Our job in spiritual growth is to cooperate with the Gardener. We receive the seed of the gospel. (James 1). Like a tree planted by streams of water that sends out its roots by the stream, we remain in a dependent relationship with God, spending time in his Word, praying, investing in his community of believers: the church (Jeremiah 17). We endure the pruning that is required to make us grow (John 15). We realize that compost is necessary for fruit production...fruit can grow out of the darkest moments of our lives. (Romans 5:3-6)

And third, the fruit of the Spirit is not about being selective. It's about all nine qualities exhibited in our personalities. When it comes to our own experience of the fruit of the Spirit, we tend to be a bit picky. We're selective. But God intends to grow all nine evidences of his character in our lives. When God is growing an example of what he looks like, he strives to illustrate all the aspects of his nature, not just the ones that tend to spring naturally from certain types of personalities.

Do a quick Fruit Inventory. Look at all nine of these characteristics that God wants to grow in our lives. Where is fruit growing? What fruit is absent?
It's not about being nice. It's about being like Jesus. It's not all up to us. It's not about being selective.

who we are precedes what we do. if we are fruit-filled people, we will live lives that reproduce fruit.

Think naked fruit. Just fruit. That's how God intended nature to reveal his character, and that's how he wants us to represent him as well. Naked fruit is advertisement enough: simple, pure, and truthful love, joy, peace, patience, kindness, goodness, faithfulness, gentleness and self-control. Fruit markets. **C**

Elisa Morgan is the president and CEO of MOPS International (**www.mops.org**), an outreach to moms with over 3,500 groups in more than 30 countries. Elisa is a sought-after speaker to varied audiences. Her many books include *Mom, You Make a Difference!* and *Naked Fruit*. A licensed minister, she resides in Colorado with her husband, Evan, her two adult children and one grandson.

PARKING LOT INTEGRITY
A DEEP TRANSFORMATION OF OUR LIVES ➡ By Mark Sanborn

INTEGRITY IS AN OFTEN-USED WORD THAT IS PROBABLY TRULY UNDERSTOOD BY FEW. LIKE JAZZ MUSIC, IT IS EASIER EXPERIENCED THAN EXPLAINED.

We bemoan a lack of integrity in our leaders but are we as critical of ourselves in this regard? After all, integrity and character often co-exist in the dark, unobserved areas of our lives. While we hear about accountability coaches, I've never heard of an integrity coach. Perhaps that is because while we can observe the exterior behavior, we can't view the interior intention.

Just what is integrity? The word is derived from the Latin word "integer" meaning "whole." The definition of integrity is "an unbroken completeness, wholeness....or incorruptibility." In short, it is the condition of being complete.

Integrity is about wholeness. Popeye alluded to the essence of integrity when he said, "I yam what I yam. Culturally we think that "what you see is what you get" is a good thing. And the current overused admonition to "keep it real" could easily mean to be who you really are and behave as who you really are.

So far so good, but consider: a thief can have more integrity than a pastor. In the crook's case his or her lawlessness could be genuine and consistent who he or she is; a pastor, in contrast, could lack this wholeness: he or she may behave incon-

sistently with the message preached last Sunday (or, in our case, inconsistent with the message we agreed with when we heard it least Sunday).

An important question, then, is this: "What kind of integrity is important?" Consider the perspective of writer Mark Halfon. He defines integrity in terms of a person's commitment to pursuing a moral life and, importantly, their responsibility in seeking to understand just what a moral life demands.

As Christians, we hold a worldview that addresses what a moral life demands. The writer of Ecclesiastes 12:13 concludes his far-reaching contemplation of life and its meaning with advice: Fear God and keep his command, for this is the whole duty of man." (NIV) There is a lot of theology is a few words there.

The contemporary dilemma of integrity isn't just to "know oneself" and behave well. Often our hearts are despicably wicked—at least mine is—and yet we choose not to indulge those dark desires. Does that mean we lack integrity? We can believe something is moral and right and grit our teeth to do that thing and still internally rebel.

I attend a mega church. The biggest challenge for me each Sunday is getting out of the parking lot without violating Christ's mandate to love one another. I believe I am a sinner saved by grace and that we all live in a fallen world. I just can't reconcile my beliefs to the egregious driving habits and heinous self-centeredness of all the other drivers rushing to get home. I believe I should extend grace (i.e. "cut other drivers some slack.") And on a good Sunday, I do extend grace (i.e. refrain from grimacing, sighing, horn-blowing and other unchristian behavior). But deep down, I'm often annoyed. Integrity in action? Only at a fairly shallow level.

I aspire to be one of those saintly sorts who is not only patient but who has mastered the art of letting others merge infinitely. The best I can offer up is letting only as many others merge as those who let me merge. Parking lot sainthood is a long way off for me.

I want to suggest something (that, should you be so inclined can be pursued more fully in Dallas Willard's book "Renovation of the Heart"): integrity is not just about believing and behaving consistently and congruently, but going deeper to answer the question "How does one live a truly good life from the inside out?" In

The New Testament tells us to be imitators of Christ. It is difficult enough to behave as he did, but the far greater challenge in a fallen world is to believe and feel as he did.

other words, how do I remove the darkness of my heart that, while not always present, seems lurking in the corner only to surface at the most surprising times. And how do I replace it with the attitude, desires and longing of Christ? That is only possible through the supernatural power of God.

The New Testament tells us to be imitators of Christ. It is difficult enough to behave as he did, but the far greater challenge in a fallen world is to believe and feel as he did.

So there is the dead skunk: a faux integrity says "This is what I believe and this is what I do" while all the time battling feelings, desires, longings and emotions to the contrary. We are not truly whole when only two legs of our three legged stool of integrity are in tact: what we believe, how we behave and a genuine desire to do what we believe.

Genuine desire is not negated by the automatic and temporary feelings that arise in a situation. I'm talking about the deep-seated longings of the heart—those things that we often don't do the hard work to understand in ourselves.

Let's call this kind of integrity "deep integrity." It is about a deep transformation that goes beyond the superficial espoused philosophy and observed behavior to the rock bottom longings and desires of our lives.

Can you see how the normal societal "integrity" misses the mark of the Gospels? When referring to our relationship to Christ, the bible uses the word "gnosis" which is an experiential kind of knowing. It suggests not simple recognition and observations, but an intimacy of experiencing the depths of another.

So deep integrity, within the Christian worldview, requires deep intimacy, with our savior and with ourselves. The Psalmist desired deep integrity when he said "Create in me a new heart..." He knew his old heart was corrupting his ability to bring desire, belief and behavior into alignment. The religious folks of any age do pretty well on beliefs and behaviors but didn't see the need for a transformed heart.

So where does that leave a next generation leader? I have often heard it said (although I can't source the research) that moral failure short-circuits more leaders than anything else. Easy integrity—saying and doing the right things—only goes

so far in sustaining a leader. If moral failures ruin leaders, a lack of deep integrity demoralizes leaders. It is evidenced by the little voice that asks "Why do I feel like an imposter? How come I still don't feel right even when what I believe and what I do are right?"

Deep integrity is aligning our hearts with our Creator's. It begins with a deep and ongoing investigation of ourselves, and the desires and longing behind what we give intellectual ascent to. It recognizes that only with God's help, over time spent in the crucible of life, we can change not only what we believe and what we do, but what we desire. Deep integrity is congruency of all three. **C**

Mark Sanborn is the president of Sanborn & Associates, Inc., an idea studio for leadership development. He is an internationally recognized speaker and author of the bestselling book *The Fred Factor: How Passion In Your Work* and *Life Can Turn the Ordinary Into the Extraordinary.* For more information check out **www.marksanborn.com**.

Transparent
Everyday Integrity

By Christine Willard

THE LIGHTS DIM, THE CAMERAS ROLL, AND THE AUDIENCE STILLS AS THE SILHOUETTE OF A WOMAN LARGER THAN LIFE ENTERS THE ARENA. NOT A WORD IS UTTERED AS ALL EYES CENTER ON THIS YOUNG LADY WHO IS SETTING THE STAGE AS A NEXT GENERATION LEADER. AS THE NIGHT DRAWS TO A CLOSE, AND THE WOMAN LEAVES THE STADIUM, SHE DRIVES AWAY FROM THE BUILDING LEFT ONLY WITH THE MEMORIES OF AN AUDIENCE HELD CAPTIVE AND PASSION IN HER SPIRIT.

The questions pounding inside her heart echo sentiments of relief, wonder, and awe. Relief that the night went smoothly, wonder at the issues raised, and awe at the grace of God that He would choose a sinner like her to lead the next generation. This woman knows exactly who she was, who she is, and who she is becoming. She has learned the secret of letting what is on the inside flow over into what is on the outside. This young woman has made it her commitment to live a life of wholeness, a life of everyday integrity.

Defining Integrity

Integrity seems to be a bygone word from the past. Oh, we speak of integrity like we read of it in a book, but our lives fail to live out the definition of its meaning. Integrity defined is the quality or condition of being whole or undivided, completeness. A next generation leader will lead by establishing a personal sense of wholeness (integrity); in other words, having the confidence of knowing we have been made complete.

Colossians 2:9-10 states, "For in Him all the fullness of Deity dwells in bodily form, and in Him you have been made complete ... " (NASB) How exciting is this verse! Basically, Paul is saying that all the fullness of the Deity that dwells in Christ (which is some crazy fullness) has been made available to us also because Christ Himself completes us! It is in this fullness that we gain our wholeness. In other words, we become leaders of integrity as we take part in the fullness of Christ.

Being complete does not indicate we are perfect; integrity does not mean a leader never makes mistakes. Rather, the focus is on having an honest heart before God and man. Our current culture is hungry for men and women who concentrate more on who they are than what they are known as. A leader knows who they are in Christ, both the good and the bad, and has come to terms with who they are in light of their completeness through the blood of Christ.

Is it possible the reason leaders fail so often in the area of integrity is because they do not understand the grace the Father offers to them? We do not have to have a perfect past, only a redeemed past. We do not have to show a perfect life, only a complete life. Integrity is making the effort to live every day in the wholeness Christ Jesus offers us. The problem, however, is that too often we allow the world's definitions and standards detract us from becoming men and women of true character.

Deterrents to Integrity

One of the greatest obstacles in becoming leaders who model integrity is that we have allowed the world to set the standard of what a true leader is. We look at the world's ideal of leadership, where the strong survive, and fail to realize we have become slaves to weakness. The book of Ecclesiastes sums up Solomon's observation of life with this important key: Fear God. Many Christian leaders today in contrast have learned to fear man, rather than God. We allow the opinion of our congregation, donors, or board of directors dictates our decisions. When it is all said and done: what we fear is what we are slave to.

Our spirit within us causes a rift between what we know we should do and what we do. We are divided because we do not fear God, rather we fear man. We cannot lead with integrity if we are divided for as the former definition shows: the very essence of integrity denotes wholeness. Next generation leaders, in contrast, are courageous enough to do the right thing. There is no division in their spirit, as they draw from the fullness of the Holy Spirit. They fear God rather than man.

Determining Priorities

How do we gain this confidence of character? We find out what matters to God and make that matter to him. True leadership concentrates more on nurturing inside character than painting outside appearances. Integrity understands that God is more concerned with matters of the heart, than the charisma or talents of a man. When it is all said and done, people are more drawn to sincerity of character than the glamour of show.

Next generation leaders make God's priorities their own and then watch these priorities play out in their everyday life. You see, there is a difference between knowing and doing. How many leaders know the right thing to do, but don't do it? We are quick to read another book, listen to another sermon, or attend another seminar but slow to actually put into practice what we already know.

Day by Day

So, when and where is the best place to practice integrity? Every day, in our homes, in our cars, at our jobs. As wives, we learn to submit to our husbands out of reverence to Christ. As husbands, we learn to love our wives as Christ loved the church. As children, we honor our parents because we know it is right.

Proverbs 12:3 says, "A man cannot be established through wickedness, but the righteous cannot be uprooted." (NIV) We will never succeed as next generation leaders if we fail to be godly leaders in our own homes, behind closed doors. It is the character we possess in our homes that ensures our credibility in public.

Dilemmas

We are living in a post-modern world that wants more than anything for one real leader to step up and be genuine. As leaders, we will be faced with issues and questions that provide no easy answers. As relativity has taken precedence, next generation leaders must balance relativity with the timelessness of fearing God. History shows that when a society is asking its toughest questions, the ground is most fertile for Christian impact through influence. Will we lead with integrity as we take part in all the fullness of Christ? Will our priorities be experienced as we fear God more than man? We can live out our integrity everyday as we concentrate less on outward status and more on inside character that is built on the wholeness of Christ. C

Being complete does not indicate we are perfect; integrity does not mean a leader never makes mistakes. Rather, the focus is on having an honest heart before God and man.

Christine Willard's passion is teaching women the Word of God. She is the founder of Redeeming Womanhood Bible Studies. Christine received her M.A.T.S. from Grace Theological Seminary and currently serves as a mental health clinician. In her free time, she loves to travel and mountain bike with her husband, Tim. For more information, **visit www.flickernail.com.**

Journal

What does UNCOMPROMISING IN INTEGRITY mean to me?

THINK

PASSIONATE about God

Am I passionately pursuing my relationship with God?

I must have awareness of my small role in God's big, developing story. This is critical to my humility, faith and trust in Him as the definer of how He will use me and my calling. To have this constant awareness, I must connect with God without ceasing through all of life, whether in study, music, art, film, vocation or relationships. My passion for God to receive Glory must be bigger than my desire for Glory.

extreme makeover
church ★ edition

By Ben Ortlip

THESE DAYS, THERE'S A BIG EMPHASIS ON MAKING THE CHURCH "CULTURALLY RELEVANT." BUT FOR MOST CHURCH LEADERS, IT'S TOO LITTLE TOO LATE. LET'S FACE IT, HOW CAN YOU BE CUTTING EDGE WHEN YOUR ORGANIZATION IS BUILT ON ANCIENT, TRADITIONAL PILLARS? NIKE HAS THE SWOOSH. MCDONALD'S HAS THE GOLDEN ARCHES. CAN YOU REALLY EXPECT TO CONNECT WITH YOUR TARGET AUDIENCE USING A TWO THOUSAND–YEAR OLD WOODEN CROSS AS A LOGO? BY ALL ACCOUNTS, IT WILL TAKE NOTHING SHORT OF AN EXTREME MAKEOVER TO BRING THE CHURCH'S PACKAGING UP TO SPEED IN THE NEW MILLENNIUM.

I can help. As a veteran media huckster, I'd like to share a few trade secrets for those of you looking to fine-tune your church's "brand" in the marketplace. You see, I've lived and worked inside the American media machine for going on three decades. In the early days, when I wasn't covering football games for a small town newspaper, I worked in a TV newsroom, monitoring police scanners for the next big story. Later, I produced and hosted a daily radio show. Then, throughout my twenty-year career in the advertising industry, I mastered the craft of manipulating an unwitting public into buying my client's brand of fast food, luxury car, soft drink, golf ball … you name it.

So when it comes to the business of being culturally relevant and influencing people groups, I can tell you how this whole game works. All you need is the right message and the right opportunity.

Incidentally, I've been thinking it's high time we ran a first-class ad for Jesus during the Super Bowl. I'm picturing Jim Caviezel pulling up in a black Hummer, "Join me for the ultimate post-game party: Heaven." We'll get Mel Gibson to direct it. We could co-op the media buy, and there'd be a 5-second local tag at the end for your church. Now that's the kind of maneuvering that could build some serious top-of-mind-awareness for the local Body!

Not that the church is doing too shabby without my great suggestions. It's getting more and more hip each week. For starters, this whole contemporary worship service thing is the bomb. Or, as we in the business used to say, it has legs. In the future, I see multiple services to cover every popular music style, from techno to R&B.

There's also a big surge in the use of video and live drama on Sunday mornings. Hey, why stay home when I can catch all the latest movie trailers from the comfort of my favorite pew? See there. You don't need an old pro like me to divulge my patented methods for influencing the crowd. A lot of churches are figuring out the formula on their own. (Oops, did I just say formula?)

I remember the first time I used the spiritual gift of hucksterism to build ministry. I was in charge of a campus ministry at the high school where my wife taught history. I had inherited a handful of church-going kids who were mostly interested in meeting other Christians. A classic holy huddle. But I was about to teach those kids a few Madison Avenue tricks! A couple of weeks later, the room was packed with attentive "seeker" teenagers. My secret? I advertised that someone would walk away one hundred dollars richer. Hey, you can't get more culturally relevant than cash, can you? Sure enough, I selected a student at random and challenged him to trust me with one dollar from his wallet. Then, using my dazzling

magician's skills, I folded the bill and handed it back to the student. When he unfolded it, he was holding a crisp $100 bill instead! Those kids were stunned. You can just imagine the clever way I weaved the Gospel message into my act.

The following week, however, we were back to our usual holy huddle and scratching our collective heads. I guess at $100 a pop, I couldn't afford to keep having that kind of impact for the kingdom.

Thinking back on that experience, I'm forced to admit that while hucksterism is great for things like attendance and Nielsen ratings, it doesn't bring a lot of life change. Sure, I had the attention of those young people. But I had no influence. To them, I was nothing more than a sideshow. Not the beacon of hope that I really wanted to be.

I can't help thinking that churches often face the same dilemma. Being culturally relevant is great. But it's not enough to earn you influence into another person's life. At least, not when it comes to sharing the mystery of the Gospel. There's something about the Gospel that refuses to be huckstered up. It can't be packaged like other brands because it's like no oth-

er brand in the marketplace. People don't buy the Gospel because it's cool. They buy it because it's real. And in culture, "cool" is the opposite of "real."

The world has lots of ways to influence the consuming public. But when it comes to church leadership, the rules are different. So at the risk of repeating something you already know, I'd like to insert a familiar thought back into the agenda of this latest movement of the church: Personal influence for God comes only from personal experience with God. It doesn't come from knowledge about God. And it certainly doesn't come from having a rock band play "Amazing Grace" on Sunday mornings.

Unless you know God personally—unless you are ready to share Him from current personal experience—then you don't really have anything to offer the lost world around you. (Ouch.) It's like the glow-in-the-dark stickers on my kid's ceiling. If the lights haven't been shining on them recently, they're just like every other piece of plastic in his room. But if the light's been on, they'll shine for hours.

Case in point: the woman at the well in John 4. Armed with nothing but a single,

authentic encounter with the Lord, she went back and captured the attention of her entire home town. They couldn't wait to see the man who'd had such an impact on this woman they knew. They were not enamored by her (she was clearly not part of the Abercrombie crowd). They were enamored by her enamoredness with Christ. "Come see the man who … " They had to see for themselves. It was pretty obvious that something amazing had happened. And who knows, it might just be what they've been secretly searching for their whole lives.

"Cool" may draw a crowd. But only "real" can draw crowds and change lives.

So go ahead and take the tour at the latest fastest-growing megachurch. Learn their patented techniques. Buy the cool video loops to use in worship. Crank up the volume on that Marshall amplifier. But don't think for a second that any of it will make you influential for Christ with your flock. If a cool environment was what they really wanted, they'd choose Starbucks over your sanctuary seven days a week. For a good movie, they'd go to Blockbuster. And as for music, they can download anything they want to hear.

The real reason people continue to drag themselves out of bed on Sunday morning is because you've got something they can't buy at Wal-Mart. It's something so profound that their souls can't rest without it. And they're banking the choicest parts of their weekend on the hope that you've actually discovered it and can show them where to find it.

That being said, there is one thing you can do to maximize your influence for Christ. Maximize your intimacy with Him. Every Christian is a walking, talking commercial for Christ. So what are you advertising? Is it all about an organization with cool programs? A lifestyle? A stance on morality? A loving community? Or are you offering people the chance to network with someone who actually knows God personally?

The most influential Christians in my life have always been the people who seemed to be close, personal friends of God.

If Jesus were to offer extreme makeovers for churches, He'd focus less on worship styles and more on what's really going on inside the hearts of the leaders.

They're the ones who gave me the mental image that Jesus is a real person … as if He just walked out of the room the minute before I walked in … and if I had arrived just a few minutes earlier, I would have actually seen Him in person.

Are you that kind of witness for Christ? Does your natural ethos reflect the impact of this relationship on your life? If you really want to be a leader for the kingdom, it needs to.

If you want a church that connects with today's culture, the first step is to make sure you've got what they're looking for. When the music fades and the sermon is over, have you been a person whom they would consider a close, personal friend of God? Can they sense your enamored-ness with Him? By getting to know you, would

they gain an insider's perspective on God Himself? The way you could get a peek inside the life of Bill Gates by talking to his mom, or Lance Armstrong by talking to one of his teammates? As a personal friend of God, you represent a bridge to Someone people are longing to meet. And who better to make a personal introduction than a close friend?

When it comes to real influence, nothing talks like real experience. You are only as influential for God as you are experienced with God. That doesn't mean you need long years of experience. But your experience must be real.

If Jesus were to offer extreme makeovers for churches, He'd focus less on worship styles and more on what's really going on inside the hearts of the leaders. So here

are three tips to cultivate real influence for Christ:

Tip #1: Practice private, authentic worship

This may sound obvious, but there's more here than you might realize. You will never be a better leader than you are a worshiper, because worship is a direct reflection of your intimacy with God. Ultimately, worship is what you're "selling." If you don't buy your own product, how can you expect to influence others to buy it?

We're not talking about putting together a great worship program or singing along on Sunday morning. We're not even talking about having your quiet time. We're talking about what happens in the privacy of your conscious thought when you wake

You will never be a better leader than you are a worshiper.

Personal influence for God comes only from personal experience with God.

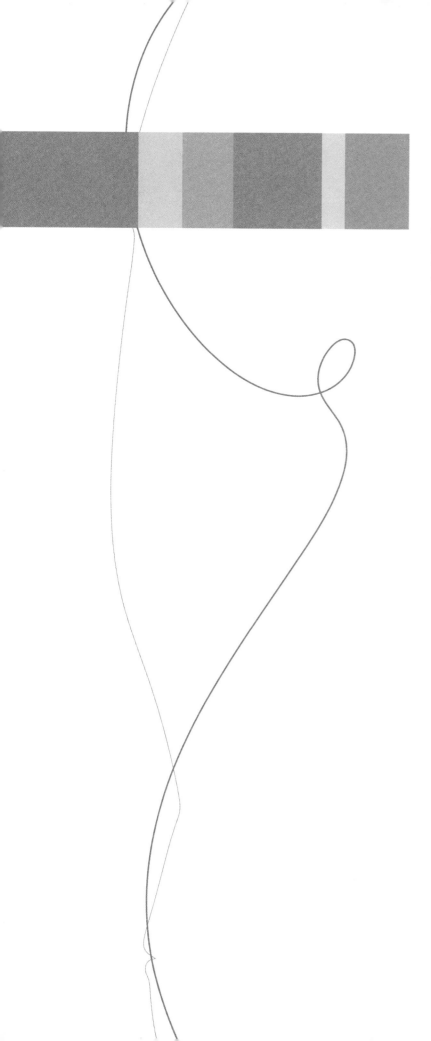

YOUR STORY

We were created for Intimacy with God. It is the passion of our souls. How do you seek God? Write a story of an experience where you felt more passionate about God than any other time of your life. Is intimacy a once-in-a-while experience or a daily walk for you? How would you encourage others to live a life of daily intimacy with God?

PRAISE HABIT

Becoming Who We Are

By David Crowder

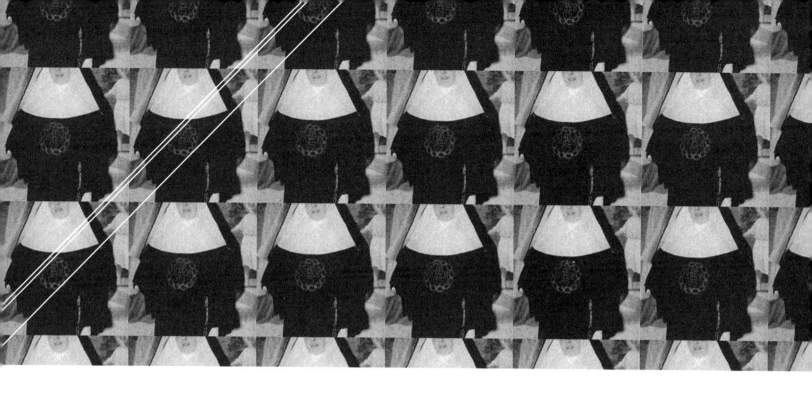

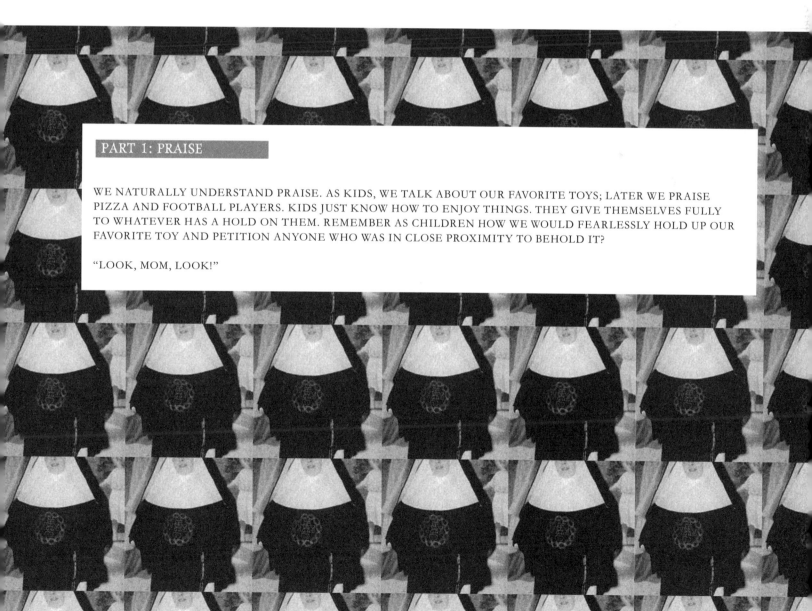

PART 1: PRAISE

WE NATURALLY UNDERSTAND PRAISE. AS KIDS, WE TALK ABOUT OUR FAVORITE TOYS; LATER WE PRAISE PIZZA AND FOOTBALL PLAYERS. KIDS JUST KNOW HOW TO ENJOY THINGS. THEY GIVE THEMSELVES FULLY TO WHATEVER HAS A HOLD ON THEM. REMEMBER AS CHILDREN HOW WE WOULD FEARLESSLY HOLD UP OUR FAVORITE TOY AND PETITION ANYONE WHO WAS IN CLOSE PROXIMITY TO BEHOLD IT?

"LOOK, MOM, LOOK!"

We instinctively knew what it was to praise something. It's always been in us. We were created for it. It's a part of who we are. As kids, we were fabulous at it. But as adults we become self conscious and awkward. Something gets lost. I think we do it to each other. At some point, I hold the toy up exultantly and you comment that it looks ridiculous to hold the toy up in such a way. It's not a cool toy like I believed it to be. It is worn and tired, you point out. And we slowly chip away at each other's protective coatings of innocence until one day we wake up and notice we are naked and people are pointing.

Occasionally, I'm watching a movie or reading words in a book or I'm walking down a street in California and the breeze on my skin feels full of water, like my arms are floating in a pool, and I'm inspired to live anew in an innocent rediscovering way I haven't thought of in a long time. Then just as I lean in to take a bite, to suck with all my might at the marrow, to breathe in with as much ferocity as I can muster, I see your eyes and hear your whispers.

"That's not polite. Use your silverware. If you don't have any we'll get you some. Please, we beg you. It is barbaric and difficult to watch. We have moved beyond this. Come with us. Please. We are becoming uncomfortable."

The moment I see a hill painted in greenest of grass, with long infinite blades waltzing in the wind, and make up my mind to sprint to the top, to give myself to gravity and let it roll me down, I hear "Dork!" shouted from behind me somewhere and I stop.

"What would they think? This is the thing of children. This is not civilized. Act your age."

This is what we have done to one another.

Think back. Try hard to recall what praise in its undiluted purity felt like. When you would dance with your arms fully extended rather than elbows bent, folded closely to your person in such a guarded fashion. Remember how effortlessly we sang the praises of things we enjoyed? It was so easy and fluid and natural. What if this kind of praise freely leaked from us in delightful response to God?

What if life were like that all the time? What if we were so moved by who God is, what He's done, what He will do, that praise, adoration, worship, whatever, continuously careened in our heads and pounded in our souls. This is what we will do for eternity. What makes us think our time on earth should be any different? What keeps it from being so?

Spent needles, cigarette butts, spitting bits of fingernail, toilet seats in the upright position ... For some reason, when I hear the word *habit* my head naturally inserts *bad* in front of it. Don't think ill of me, please. In my defense, I just took a quick survey of those sitting within the proximity of my voice in Barnes & Noble and four out of five said "bad" when I asked what they thought of when they heard the word *habit*. Habits like drinking milk from the carton, cussing, buying Top 40 music, killing things, grinding teeth, clicking a pen over and over and over, cleaning ears with sharp instruments like, say, keys or a light saber, burning things that look flammable, sleeping while driving. It's incredible the things that become habitual.

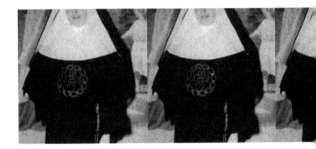

THAT THING YOU DO

A habit is an act acquired by experience and performed regularly and automatically. A habit is influenced not only by elements that bring the behavior about but also by rewards or punishments that follow the behavior.[1] Habits involve no conscious choice among alternatives.

THE GOOD, THE BAD, AND ...

It seems for most bad habits we display, there was never any intentional formation. Most alcoholics do not sit down and think, "Okay, just twenty-one days and I'll need this stuff like water." Most nail biters do not think, "I love the taste of my fingernails and the feeling of tearing them down to the quick. I really need to consider doing it more often." No, usually destructive habits are formed more subtly with very little thought and planning.

Good habits seem more difficult to manage. Maybe it's just me, but things like brushing your teeth, exercising, proper eating, saying "yes, sir" and "no, sir," and sending Mother's Day flowers seem much harder to acquire than, say, burping at the table. Why does it seem like the

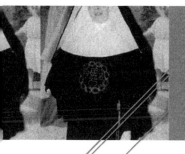

> What if we were so moved by who God is, what He's done, what He will do, that praise, adoration, worship, whatever, continuously careened in our heads and pounded in our souls.

formation must be much more intentional in our adoption of good habits?

I'm convinced it's because we are bent, deficient, broken. Things aren't right. Things aren't as they were at the start. Innocence is gone, and left alone in our depraved state we tend to choose destructive paths. Oh, we have choice. We have will, this capacity to choose among alternative courses of action and to act on the choice made. But good habits seem counterintuitive. When we do find the will and courage to head down that narrow path, we often find that even then we still have a deep capacity for taking beautiful things and turning them into hideous remnants of what was intended.

For instance, we want to exercise more or eat healthier, so we set out to develop routines that help us accomplish this. Then one day we find ourselves standing in front of a mirror, flexing, and realize we've been doing this for the last thirty minutes. It dawns on us that we've become complete narcissists. Okay. Sorry. Bad example. That's never happened to

me, either. I actually avoid mirrors for the most part and have only flexed on three occasions in my life, all occurring before the age of ten. Let me try again.

Countless times I have tried to develop a habit of having a "quiet time." Sometimes it would stick. Sometimes it would not. Guilt would be thick when it would not. But for a long period it became what I did first thing every day. *It was beauty. The internal joy it brought was overwhelming.* Then at some point it went hollow. It's not that it was a bad idea to form a habit of a quiet time, but the habit had slyly begun to suck the life out of my relationship with God. I had fallen in love with my spirituality rather than with the one whom I sought, and in the end it left me void and wanting.

A frightening aspect of habit attached to our spiritual formation is that inherent in the idea of habit is the possibility for meaningless ritual. With the formation of habit there is a subtle abdication of consciousness in our actions. This can

twist things that were intended to bring life into cold and empty ritualistic experiences. Indeed we are broken. We do bad things without thinking and when we try to do good things they often end up warped. How can we maintain life in our spiritual formation?

TAKE ME BACK TO THE START

Remember the start? Our beginnings? In the beginning there was the recognition that the source of all things was Creator God. There was relational communion with our Maker in all that was life, and we were alive, really alive. He was in the breeze and under rocks and in our love and in our skin and in His voice, oh, His voice. There was no knowledge of anything but what was good, and gratefulness beat in our bones. This is the kind of praise that is sweeter and stronger than anything conjured up in an order of worship on Sunday or during our scheduled morning quiet time or in the songs of the "contemporary worship" service Saturday evening or in classrooms of scholarly study.

My intent here is not to tear away at spiritual disciplines or discard them as dated contrivances but to inject some portion of freedom and life into them. It is my belief that we were made to praise and that the original intentions for it might have been bigger and sweeter than most of us have dreamed or that a scheduled moment could properly contain. We find ourselves in a dynamic, fluid relationship with the divine, where there is such a perpetual movement and flow that a static, formulaic approach undermines and lessens what could exist. It is hamburger stuck in our esophagus. We were meant for every moment to be fully alive with this dynamic relating and vibrant presence of hope in finding our Maker near us. Again, nothing is non-spiritual. Grasping this does not diminish the necessity of our disciplines; it only brings to them more depth and beauty.

There's a cycle that takes place where we find/experience a spiritual habit that brings connection and meaning, but eventually even that thing will get stale and something else will need to find its way in. We need to continually redefine what our spiritual disciplines look like, an importunate redefining of the habits that define us. There is inherent danger in ritual, but there is still the necessity in our movement toward Christ and His intentions for our lives. There is the definitive need for a continual shedding of depravity and the taking on of His righteousness. There is the need for us to embrace this new way of living that is found in the person of Christ. Or perhaps it's more than that: allowing His life to engulf and cover us. We must continually seek ways to place ourselves in this embrace.

The spiritual life is first of all a life. It is not merely something to be known and studied, it is to be lived.
THOMAS MERTON
THOUGHTS IN SOLITUDE

There is risk in placing yourself in the way of His embrace. Richard Foster speaks of spiritual disciplines in the illustrative terms of a path on a trepidatious ledge set between two sheer drop-offs. On one side is the danger of a works-based legalism and on the other an abyss of a faith devoid of action.[2] But the path is life; it is real living.

So here is the process I propose for putting our understanding of habit in terms of the spiritual formation of praise into new words:

What if we added another definition of habit to our ideas of natural versus formed that might move us beyond our sterile idea of ritual or our paralyzed state of legalistic fear and help us rediscover what was meant to be second nature? I dug around a little and found that the word *habit* has its roots in Middle English, "clothing," Old French, "clothing, behavior custom," and ultimately, in the Latin word *habitus*, which means "condition, character" and *habere*, meaning "to have, to hold." With a tad more linguistic study I discovered that at one point in history, habit became particularly associated with a distinctive dress or costume, especially of a religious order.[3] This I liked. As soon as I read that definition, a memory of Audrey Hepburn in the movie *The Nun's Story* came quickly in, flooding thought.

In the 1959 movie *The Nun's Story*, Audrey was not dressed so fashionably chic as was her big-screen custom. No, in this cinematic feature she donned the habit of a religious sister. Due to the universality of the Catholic Church, when we hear the word *nun*, images of starched linen headbands and wimples, long heavy dresses, and gracefully dripping black veils come to mind. Granted, for some this image represents a dated way of living for the fashionable nun on the go, but for many this characteristic black-and-white dress is a symbol of holiness — a redolent icon that has been a definitive portrait of the Catholic Church for nearly two thousand years. A few of you might have also found thoughts of the Nunzilla wind-up toy or the ever-popular Fighting Nun puppet dancing in your head, but the reason those are so humorous is due to the cultural stigma that nuns have within our society. Their way of life is so mysterious and *other-than* the typical Western consumerist experience. To see a nun in full habit is so visually compelling, I am usually stopped in my tracks and found lingering to watch their movements and interactions.

One particularly searing encounter innocuously occurred in Times Square, NYC. Amid the bright lights and store windows satiated with color, there they

We find ourselves in a dynamic, fluid relationship with the divine, where there is such a perpetual movement and flow that a static, formulaic approach undermines and lessens what could exist.

were, impossible to miss, in glorious black and white. Two women lost in conversation. It is a most haunting thing to observe such visual contrasts unfurl in front of you. The habit demands attention and will not let go. What is this life they have chosen? How do you put that thing on? What is a wimple anyway? In *The Nun's Story* there is a scene where Audrey Hepburn's character participates in the clothing ceremony that was once common for all sisters entering the devout life. During the ceremony, the sister would receive her consecrated garb and new religious name. She would then lie flat on the ground before the altar as a black funeral pall was placed over her and candles burned at each corner of her body. The choir would sing a sequence from a requiem Mass, symbolizing her death to self. Her old life was gone. What was before this moment had vanished. A new name, a new set of clothes, and a new way of living had begun.

By the tenth century, the ceremony closely resembled an elaborate "secular" marriage service with a silver ring placed on the nun's finger and her recitation of, "I am espoused to Him Whom angels serve; whose beauty sun and moon behold with wonder."

In her book *The Habit: A History of the Clothing of Catholic Nuns*, Elizabeth Kuhns writes:

For these nuns, the habit is a wearable sacramental with a supernatural character that cannot be replicated in secular clothing... It is important to remember that clothing is a uniquely human characteristic, a silent but powerful medium from which we can learn who we are and what we value. Clothing defines gender, status, beauty, and ideology, and it can be found in virtually every culture. It touches on human history, psychology, sociology, economics, aesthetics, technology, customs, laws, attitudes, and values... The habit has the glamour of fashion while being antifashion ... The sighting of a nun in habit remains for most of us a notable event, because what the habit proclaims is something so counterculture and so radical, we cannot help but to react with awe and reverence or with suspicion and disdain.[4]

This is the kind of Praise Habit I wish to pursue. It is the one we already have on, the one we find ourselves in.

In our encounter with Christ we, too, have been laid down, devastated by His grace. We have been covered by this same grace. We have been taken from death to life by this grace. Our identity is changed. What was before this new beginning has vanished. We have been given new clothes. We have put on Christ. We are found dressed in His rescue, redemption, and righteousness and, aware of this rescue, we spew forth praise. We wear this very rescue into our relationships, into our interactions with pals and family and work and play. It is present in our embodiments or neglections of justice, in our contention or ignore-ance of the poor, of the widows, of the sick, of those in need. To wear the rescue of Christ into every moment is for every moment to become alive with the possibility of revelation. With the aware-ness of rescue, things unsuspected will begin to revelate redemption.

What choice is there but to respond in praise? Praise is fundamentally a responding to the initiations and intimations of God. The way of *living praise* sets out to find God's revelation, to carry God's intentions for His creation into our everyday comings and goings. And this way of life should be so compelling and mysterious and other-than that people see us coming from a long way off and it stops them in their tracks and they wait and watch just to see our exchanges and wonder at this life that has been chosen and how to put it on and what is this deeper, truer way of living anyway?

A nun does not get up each morning and go to the closet and think to herself, *Hmmm. I wonder what to wear today.* The habit is what she wears. It is what covers her. It is what identifies her. Our condition is the same. Our habit is the Christ. He is what covers us. He is what identifies us. We wear Him into every moment, and when we live with this awareness, we PRAISE CHRIST. **C**

Exerpted from Praise Habit: Finding God in Sunsets and Sushi *by David Crowder, copyright 2004. Used by permission of NavPress –* **www.navpress.com**. *All rights reserved.*

1. "Habit," Microsoft® Encarta® Encyclopedia 99. © *1993-1998 Microsoft Corporation. All rights reserved.*
2. Richard J. Foster, Celebration of Discipline *(San Francisco: Harper San Francisco, 1988), p.8.*
3. Dictionary.com, s.v. "habit."
4. Kuhns, p.7.

David Crowder is the pastor of music and arts at University Baptist Church in Waco, Texas, where he lives with his wife, Toni. A talented musician and worship leader, he has released three CDs on the sixstepsrecords/EMI CMG label. *Praise Habit* is his first book. (**www.davidcrowderband.com**)

A LIFETIME OF LESSONS FROM HOWARD HENDRICKS

KIERKEGAARD ONCE SAID, "LIFE MUST BE LIVED FORWARD, BUT IT CAN ONLY BE EVALUATED BACKWARDS."

These are some of the convictions that I have developed in my 65 years of the faith and 56 years in public ministry. This is a highly personal, refined study that I hope will provoke your thinking.

THE PARAMOUNT IMPORTANCE OF PERSONAL SPIRITUAL DISCIPLINES

In Philippians 1:9, the Apostle Paul prays that our "love may abound more and more in knowledge and depth of insight." There are many ways in which to do this. I have chosen four of them:

BIBLE STUDY AND MEMORY PROGRAM

The two options confronting a Christian: you are in the Word conforming to Christ, or you are in the world being squeezed into its mold. I had a seminary professor that made one statement that has changed the course of my life. He

said, "Do not study for a course. Study for a lifetime of ministry." I left that class and developed a program that I continue using to this day. I spend one hour every day in a personal study of the Word of God. I would substitute nothing for that commitment. It has revolutionized every aspect of my life and ministry.

PRAYER

There is only one question the disciples ever asked the Lord in terms of teaching. "Lord, teach us to pray?" (Luke 11: 1 KJV) They did not ask Him why they should pray. Every time they found Jesus, they found Him on His knees. They began to discover that it was the secret to His ministry. We need to make a decision that prayer is the key to our ministry. You are gifted, trained, and experienced. Use these, but do not depend on them.

PERSONAL EVANGELISM

If you spend all of your time around Christians, your faith will die. The gospel is failing today not for a lack of power but for a lack of audience. I can't recall a single verse of scripture that commands a lost person to go to church, but I know many verses that command believers to penetrate the lost world.

SOLITUDE

Two things that are difficult to keep in balance, particularly in ministry, are the involvement with people and isolation from people. You cannot continue to be around people and continue to impact them. One of the greatest challenges in a hurried society is getting alone with the Lord. Let's face it; if you don't hear from heaven, you have nothing to say to your generation.

THE MANAGEMENT OF OUR TIME

While we do not all have the same personality and giftedness, we all have only 24 hours in a day. Jesus only had 24 hours, and he never rushed. Make sure that you are investing your time. It is the most important commodity. Wasting it is like wasting eternity.

Our schedules, though, must be flexible. If your schedule cannot be interrupted, you do not have a schedule, you have a straight jacket. In the book of Mark, you'll find that Jesus was constantly interrupted in the midst of prayer and ministry. Interruptions are invitations to meet the needs of hurting people.

DEVELOPING A STRATEGIC NETWORK

It is fascinating to look at the outline for developing a strategic network in the New Testament. In Colossians and Romans, there are lists of individuals who impacted the Apostle Paul's ministry. Paul never assumed that he was a rugged individualist who was going to pull this off alone. He knew he needed a team.

It is important to spend time with people of different backgrounds. Spend time with people who have totally different lifestyles, convictions, religions and philosophies. No one person is as smart as all of us.

MAINTAINING BALANCE IN LIFE AND MINISTRY

Have you discovered the peril of the pendulum? Whenever you react against anything, you invariably end up with another extreme. Everyone who appears to be balanced is simply going through the center on his or her way to another extreme.

We have to determine what we will go to the mat for. I have a basic principle for this: when scripture speaks, I speak; when scripture does not speak, I do not speak. I believe this principle will give you the maturity and a legacy that lasts.

FORMATION OF CORE VALUES

These are the five values that determine everything I do.

1. OBJECTIVE What do I want the result to be at the end of my life?
2. PRIORITIES What price am I willing to pay? Many of us get lost here.
3. SCHEDULE Your schedule is a practical way of maintaining your priorities so you can accomplish your objectives.
4. DISCIPLINE Is there any area of your life in which you know you are not under the control of the Spirit?
5. COMPONENT EVALUATION What is the outcome? What are my strengths and weaknesses? What needs to change? No matter how good you are, you can be better.

COMMITMENT TO CONTINUING EDUCATION

Philippians 4:8 gives the divine curriculum, "Think on these things." (KJV) What are you studying? Most would agree that we can go somewhere to get a degree, but the question is did we get an education. Here are five areas for evaluation:

Reading

If you can read and do not read, you are no better off than someone who cannot read at all. Read literature that will stretch you. Read widely and wisely.

Listening Skills

This is the hardest skill. A person can listen 4-10 times as fast as a person can speak. That gives you a lot of extra time on your hands.

Courses and Seminars

I get more insight as to why people are doing what they are doing today from one university course a year than from most books I read.

Asking Questions

Ask penetrating questions, because one day you are going to have to come up with the answers to them.

Time to Think

Thinking is not a luxury for a leader. You must find another reason to get alone for this valuable practice.

NECESSITY OF NOT BELIEVING YOUR PRESS REPORTS

In more than 50 years at seminary, I have seen people who are gifted beyond description but never amounted to anything. Why? It's not because they failed but because they were too successful. Don't peak too soon.

For your ministry to be successful, God has to be able to trust you. When He does, do not be surprised if He gives you the quality of ministry you could only dream of.

When you see your life from the end looking backward, what will you feel? Will you die without fulfillment? I am a totally fulfilled human being. God has given me the gift of teaching, and I have spent 50 years pouring my life into people who have gone far beyond anything I could ever do. I am doing what God has called me to do. That is my passion, and it is my desire for you. **C**

Howard G. Hendricks is Chairman of the Center for Christian Leadership and Distinguished Professor at Dallas Theological Seminary. For 54 years he has touched the lives of thousands of students at Dallas Theological Seminary. He has written or co-written numerous books including *As Iron Sharpens Iron, Living by the Book, Color Outside the Lines*, and his newest release *Heaven Help the Home Today*. Married to Jeanne Hendricks for 58 years, he and his wife have raised 4 children and are proud grandparents of six granddaughters.

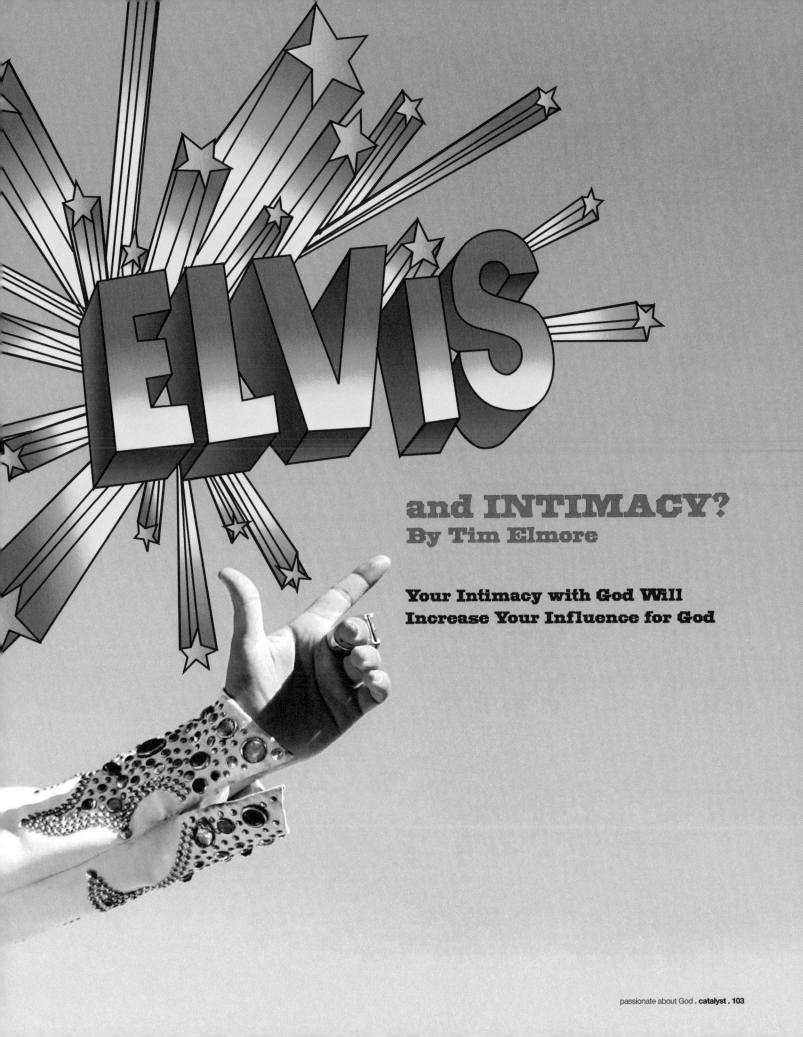

ELVIS

and INTIMACY?
By Tim Elmore

**Your Intimacy with God Will
Increase Your Influence for God**

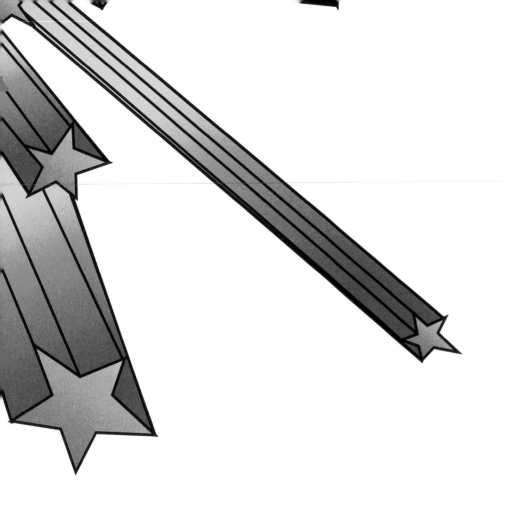

IT WAS UNDOUBTEDLY THE MOST INTRIGUING ARTICLE I HAD READ IN A LONG TIME.

EVIDENTLY, ELVIS PRESLEY WAS MAKING ANOTHER COMEBACK. A FEW YEARS AGO, A PRESLEY LOOK-ALIKE CONTEST TOOK PLACE IN NEW ENGLAND AND THE *BOSTON GLOBE* WAS THERE TO COVER IT. THEY RAN A STORY WHICH SPOTLIGHTED A DISILLUSIONED FAN NAMED DENNIS WISE. HIS COMMENTS ARE REVEALING:

"Elvis Presley was and is my idol. I've seen his concerts, I have every album he's recorded, and watched every movie he's made. I once got a hair contour like his, and now I have a face-lift that looks just like him … I have won Elvis look-alike contests dozens of times … I have ticket stubs and clippings from programs around the world; I even own some Elvis pillows from Japan.

"I wanted him to see me, so I would often storm the stage, during and after the concerts he would do. I don't think he ever noticed me. I once even climbed the walls around Graceland, the Presley mansion, to catch a glimpse of him. I think it might have been him wandering through the house as I looked through my binoculars, but I'm not sure. What an irony. It's actually funny. All the effort I put into following him … and I never could seem to get close."

Do you hear the despondency in his words? Here's a fan who began following Elvis with high expectations and ended with low fulfillment. You might call it raw disappointment. The words are haunting: "I don't think he ever noticed me…I never could seem to get close."

After reading this, I immediately thought about my relationship with God. I wonder how many times I've felt this way about God over the years—much less been bold enough to admit it. And I am a leader! I've led Bible studies, prayed, preached, fasted, sang the songs, and even lifted my hands to Him. Yet, if I'd get honest about it, at times I've felt the same way Dennis Wise felt about his idol, Elvis: "All the effort I put into following Him … and I never could seem to get close."

INTIMACY...

Intimacy. People are talking about it more and more these days. Intimacy in marriages. Intimacy among friends. And most of all—intimacy with God. We seek relationships that fulfill our need for it. We'll substitute artificial means to receive the comfort it brings. I've found that people long to experience God in a genuine way and will follow leaders who create a place for that to happen. So why is intimacy so elusive? Why is it so hard to pass on? Why do leaders struggle with this issue? What makes this fundamental need so difficult to meet?

I think there are three fundamental reasons why leaders struggle with intimacy with God:

* *The idea of intimacy with God is mystical and subjective. It's hard to measure.*
* *We battle with our own personal intimacy with God. We can't give what we don't have.*
* *We suffer from the common occupational hazards of the ministry profession.*

Listed below are four "occupational hazards" that spiritual leaders often face. All of these hazards hinder our relationship with God. They are harmful and are extremely easy to fall into. They're like danger zones. If we linger in these danger zones for more than a brief season of time, our relationship with our Heavenly Father begins to erode.

THE STARVING BAKER

We're too busy providing bread for others to eat.
It is the number one occupational hazard of Christian leadership. As a spiritual "baker," our life can become so consumed with "baking bread" for others that we don't have the time or desire to feed ourselves. We begin to replace personal quiet time with God with preparation for Bible studies, worship times, or other programs. The short-term result is that we feed others while starving ourselves. We read for program, not for personal growth. The long-term result is we become so spiritually deficient that we lose the ability to even feed other people.

THE SUPERFICAL CELEBRITY

We keep others at a distance, including God.
We live in a culture of celebrities and stars. Even in Christian circles, the one up front is a "sage on the stage." Unfortunately, as a spiritual "superficial celebrity," we may portray ourselves as unapproachable. I fell into this trap at my first church trying to guard myself from being hurt or manipulated or being discovered as an imperfect leader. To maintain this masquerade, we may keep both God and others at a distance. We diminish our ability to impact anyone else's life because we won't allow them to get close enough to see through our superficial veneer.

THE POLISHED PERFORMER

We're overly concerned with the "show" we do.
As Christian "polished performers," we often feel the need to impress others with how spiritual we are. As we become better at "playing the spiritual game," we appear to be deeper and might even be treated as godly, spiritual leaders. In reality, we may be far from that. But we're focused more on appearance than reality. If we perform long enough, we may find it hard to ever be genuine with God again. In the end, we suffer due to the distance in our relationship with God. Sadly, we often don't notice what's happened because we are so caught up with our "show" on the platform.

THE SPIRITUAL PROFESSIONAL

We perceive spirituality as our job.
As a spiritual "professional," we view our relationship with God and others as our job. Similar to the starving baker, we attempt to feed others something we're not consuming ourselves. Those who are involved in ministry, whether as a volunteer or as a pastor, are most susceptible to this. Our spirituality becomes a 9 a.m. to 5 p.m. deal, or an "every Sunday" event where we try to turn on our relationship with God on demand. Since people expect us to be "spiritual," we fall into the trap of saying the right spiritual cliché at the right time to meet those expectations. Our life is no longer filled with genuine love for God, but rather with appropriate expressions of spirituality.

Defining Intimacy

Intimacy with God can be difficult to understand because it often seems ambiguous. The New Testament provides us with some defining thoughts on what it means:

To love God and be loved by Him without fear of rejection. It is the pursuit of God in order to experience the PROMISE of Ephesians 3:18-19 and the COMMAND of Matthew 22:37, which results in the FRUIT of John 15:15-16.

Intimacy with God requires work. Salvation and spiritual intimacy is a lot like a wedding and a marriage. The wedding is relatively simple, like our conversion experience. It can happen in a moment. Experiencing intimacy with God, however, is like a marriage. It is the process of investing time and commitment. Salvation (our "position in Christ") is free. Intimacy ("abiding in Christ") is expensive. Like a good marriage. At times, intimacy with God is even tougher than marriage.

Real Life

I had a missionary friend who was frequently called away from home. It was tough on his family, but it was hardest for his little son. At the train station, the boy would cling to him as if to beg him not to go. Most of the time his dad would appease the boy by bringing him an apple (apples were a rare treat in this country). This would distract the child until after he was able to jump on the train and depart.

One day, when he knew the trip would be especially long, my friend brought two apples to the station. He knew it would be a tough departure. Sure enough, the little boy clamped onto his dad's hand with all of his might. Outside of the passenger car my friend was to board, he said, "Now son, I'm going to be home soon, I promise. And guess what? I brought you not one, but two apples."

He jammed them into his son's tiny hands and quickly hopped onto the train. After setting down his luggage, he glanced out the door to see if his son was still there. As he looked out the opening of the train, he saw the child still standing in the same place he had left him. The apples had been dropped onto the concrete and he had tears rolling down his cheeks. He heard his little boy whimper, "But daddy, I don't want your apples ... I want you."

I think God is looking for people that will say to Him, "Your answers to prayer are wonderful. Thanks for all you've given me. But even if I never got another answer, it would be enough to just know You." It's a pure desire for God. Nothing more. Nothing less. Nothing else. No hidden agendas. Is this your heart's cry?

So what can you do? You can look to Ephesians for the inner plan and Acts for the outer one. You can claim them as your biblical templates for rethinking and reconstructing a church for your neighborhood and your century. It's not going to be easy. It's a high-risk, high-reward venture to redesign the wineskins to hold the new wine we have to offer. Let's examine a few of the questions that must be confronted.

Is the Foundation Solid?

It's worth carefully considering your church's commitment to those old apostles and prophets. They've never failed us yet, and twenty centuries is a long time. Many church leaders today are infatuated with the contemporary literature of the business culture. Books like Malcolm Gladwell's *The Tipping Point* and Thomas Friedman's *The World is Flat: A Brief History of the Twenty-First Century* provide us with helpful new paradigms for understanding a rapidly changing world. But the world has always been changing, and that itself won't change. Like Odysseus shackling himself to the mast, we have to keep every element of our corporate being tied to the immutable laws of Scripture.

Challenge: *Examine the inner activities of your church for the next two weeks. How closely connected is each function to some biblical mandate? How many of the urgent biblical mandates are being attended to? To what extent is your fellowship a product of your biblical agenda?*

Is the Cornerstone Connected?

Paul identifies the church as the body of Christ, with our spiritual gifts defining his hands, his feet, his eyes, and so on. We are connected to one another through our complementary gifts and functions that serve the same purpose in unity. When most of us examine the factions, rifts, and disconnections in the typical subculture of a church, we realize how far we have strayed from this simple model. Yet when we all begin to focus on Christ, our differences have a way of vaporizing. Does his personhood and presence draw you together in fellowship? Are your people in the process of being individually transformed to his image? There is no church in this world that wouldn't be upgraded simply by refocusing on the reality of Christ.

Challenge: *Measure the intensity by which Christ has been preached, taught, and modeled in your congregation over the last twelve months. How many sermon series have focused directly on him, and how many on more listener-friendly "lifestyle" topics? Remember the dictum, "What you win them with is what you win them to." And never forget that Christ is the most powerful and attractive content we can possibly offer. Now try this one: List the 20 or 40 most influential individuals in your church. How many are directly using their spiritual gifts? In how many cases do they/you know their spiritual gifts?*

Are the Bricks Bonding?

How would you evaluate your own success in finding a sense of community? Do you find deep, satisfying human relationships within and even without the spiritual core? Can visitors feel the Spirit of God making his home in the brickwork? It's not a question of having the world's greatest preacher, hottest worship band, and most creative program. A Broadway musical or a rock concert can get the same effect. When God shows up, there is no question about the source of joy and intensity. There is no possibility of in-fighting over church politics. People simply begin to worship.

Challenge: *Do you have two friends outside your home whom you truly trust—who minister to your own needs? As for your larger group, how many pockets of* koinonia *are ablaze? When was the last time there was a sense of true, powerful community there? When was the last time a petty conflict resolved itself into tighter love and unity between the two parties (the evidence of Christ's presence)?*

Is it a Full-Body Experience?

The Acts 2:42 church—the one that "enjoyed the favor of all the people"—met the needs of body, soul, mind, and emotion. That pretty well covers it, doesn't it? Most churches today are heavily invested in one or perhaps two of these categories. You engage them all when you become truly concerned about individuals, and when you allow others to serve you. Think of your spouse, your children, your significant friendships. You don't need to check off a list, because you love them and you naturally move to meet whatever need they have at the moment. Your Forever Family should fall no lower than that ideal. What would happen if people began to walk into your church to find their hopes, desires and cravings truly satisfied? Is your congregation capable of providing that kind of love? How about through the power of Christ? The second question makes a lot of difference, doesn't it?

Challenge: *What would be the first step in reinventing your fellowship to be one that builds itself "upon the Word, through the Son, to the people, unto the Father"? What are your personal needs? Who will help you? When will you begin?*

A Community of Influence

Do you have a vision for becoming a city set on a hill? Do you have a personal community of individuals with whom you share the ups and downs of life? Imagine your church with the impact of the believers in Acts 2. It may seem like a faraway goal—like winning the lottery. But it's actually the simple mandate of every assembly where Christ is loved and followed. We have the resources we need, because God has assured us again and again in the Scripture that he will go with us, and he will empower us. Given that promise, we cannot fail—for he is the one with the greatest influence of all. **C**

Rob Suggs is an author living in Atlanta, Georgia. He has written several books and co-authored with Bruce Wilkinson, David Jeremiah, Lee Strobel, and others. You can learn more about his work at **www.robsuggs.com**

For Group Discussion:

Use these questions and journal pages to reflect and respond to what you've just read.

1. Which of the building materials for supernatural fellowship is most difficult to apply? Why?

2. According to Ephesians 2, how are Father, Son, and Holy Spirit each involved in our supernatural community?

3. Since your body, too, is a temple of the Holy Spirit (1 Corinthians 6:19), how do you need to personally apply the principles of Ephesians 2 to your own life?

4. *What can you do to enhance your own social nutrition? How can your significant extra-family relationships be enriched?*

5. *What can you specifically do this week to help rebuild your local fellowship according to God's architectural plans?*

6. *With whom are you sharing your life in community?*

DEEP DIVE

Download a complete smallgroup leader's guide at **www.catalystgroupzine.com**

For more on unity and God's desired for us to live as a community of Christ-followers, check out Ephesians 2:11-22 and Acts 2.

Ethos (n.) The fundamental character of a culture; the underlying sentiment that i[nforms] beliefs, customs, and practices of a group [...] The distinguishing character or dispositi[on of a com]munity, group, or person. To simplify, an [ethos is] expressed through spontaneous, recurring patterns.

THE STORY OF YOUR COMMUNITY

By Erwin Raphael McManus

"I'VE BECOME CONVINCED OVER THE YEARS AND THROUGH EXPERIENCE THAT THE PRIMARY ROLE OF A LEADER IS TO CREATE AND SHAPE ETHOS."

*– Quoted by Erwin Raphael McManus at Catalyst 2002
in his speech entitled the Primal Essence of Leadership.*

If a worldview is the way a community *sees* reality, then an ethos is the way a community *feels* reality. Ethos is what happens when many individuals make autonomous choices that create a unified movement. Ethos moves us when nothing else will and like nothing else will. Ethos can be described as a tribal emotion. Like emotions fire us up, ethos is the tribal fire. Ethos is the fuel of our caring and the fire of our passions. Ethos is the e-motion of a community.

Uniting a crowd into a community requires spiritual leadership, and what emerges in the process is the generation of a common culture built upon commonly held beliefs, values, and worldviews. There is no more significant reason to be a pastoral leader than to awaken an apostolic ethos. To embrace the God-given task of connecting the local church to the first-century church is an extraordinary responsibility. But God has already placed within the body of Christ everything we need to ignite the flames of spiritual revival and revolution. If local churches are essentially spiritual subcultures waiting to become cultural revolutions, then we as spiritual leaders need to engage our environment as cultural architects.

In every culture you'll find essential metaphors that define and shape its ethos. Your symbols hold your secret stories. The metaphor causes an eruption of images, ideas, dreams, beliefs, and convictions all at one time. The story of an entire people can be contained in one symbol. A culture often has two or three symbols that are fundamental to the identity of the people.

THE IMAGES OF THE INVISIBLE GOD

God has placed as a center point in the Christian movement metaphors that, once unwrapped, begin to transform not only the hearts of its constituency, but the entire ethos of the community. The central metaphor of the Christian faith is the cross. Rich with passion and purpose, the cross evokes the kind of e-motion that transforms a church into a movement. For followers of Jesus Christ, the cross becomes more than a reminder of his sacrifice, death, and resurrection. It also serves as an invitation to deny ourselves, take up our crosses, and follow him. This central metaphor of the church demands sacrifice and servanthood: The only way to live in the kingdom of God is to first die to yourself.

If this were not enough, the essence of this metaphor is reinforced with another Christian metaphor, baptism. Baptism is a water grave. It is yet another reminder of Jesus Christ's death, burial, and resurrection. Every individual who becomes a part of the Christian community must personally declare his or her own death, burial, and resurrection in a very peculiar and extraordinary way. Every follower of Jesus Christ goes to his or her grave and then lives.

And there is even a third metaphor in the movement of Jesus Christ. It is the Lord's Supper—the ongoing ordinance of the church. We revisit this metaphor over and over again. Should we be surprised that when we unwrap this third metaphor, it goes back to the same essence, passion, and purpose of the first two? The Lord's Supper is done in memory of Jesus' suf-fering, death, and resurrection. The bread being his body broken for us; the cup, his blood shed on our behalf. Jesus commanded us to do this in remembrance of him. And in the same way we are called to die to ourselves. Paul said it like this: "To live is Christ and to die is gain." (Philippians 1:21b NIV) In Galatians 2: 20-21 he explains: "I have been cruci-fied with Christ and I no longer live, but Christ lives in me. The life I live in the body, I live by faith in the Son of God, who loved me and gave himself for me. I do not set aside the grace of God, for if righteousness could be gained through the law, Christ died for nothing!" (NIV)

It is inescapable that the ethos of the New Testament church is wrapped around the concepts of sacrifice and conquest. It is a call to life through death. The apostolic leader unwraps these three metaphors and reignites the fire that burned in the first-century church. Their church erupted under the shadow of the cross. One by one, Jesus' first followers joined Jesus in his death. Church by church, they celebrated at his table. And generation by generation, through dying to themselves, Christians brought the life of Christ to the nations.

As powerful as these metaphors are, it is not enough to simply uphold them in memory of what Jesus did. It is absolutely essential to understand these metaphors if we are to shape the heart and values of the contemporary church. The metaphors not only root us in the past, but they also guide and shape our future.

While every local church uses central metaphors from the culture of *the* Church, we need to be acutely aware of the sub-metaphors that we create in our local churches. Many times the names of our churches become our metaphors. An icon in our worship or structure can become a metaphor. Designations such as Family Church, Bible Church, Community Church, or Baptist Church often have more power in shaping the ethos of our local churches than even the metaphors given to us by our Lord.

METAPHORS NOT ONLY ROOT US IN THE PAST, BUT THEY ALSO GUIDE AND SHAPE OUR FUTURE.

THE ART OF THE STORY

Wrapped up in the metaphors of a community are the stories. Every culture has stories that are wrapped up in their religion, their mythology, or their folklore. Stories retell the lives and experiences of gods or heroes. These stories do more than entertain; they inform. They are interwoven with the beliefs and ideals of the society. Stories both define and direct. In many ways, a culture's story is the story of everyone in that culture. It's the story that describes the life of the society. It's the story that describes the desired life of each individual. Leaders must choose their stories carefully. Of course, in this we Christians have an advantage. The Bible is full of great stories, and locked within those stories are the core values that God desires to pass on to his people.

Ultimately, the Bible is one great story. It is the story of God's activity in human history, both of his creation of all that exists and of his redemption of his people. This story is so big, so rich, and so profound that it requires many stories to be wrapped around it to give it proper texture and depth. Apostolic leaders are great storytellers, and they make sure that the great story is central in shaping the ethos of the community.

The church was born out of stories. The first-century church was driven by the narrative. There was no New Testament; there were no Gospels to transmit the story of Jesus. His story was entrusted to storytellers. The Christian faith grew through story—not text. Only later did the stories become Scripture. While the Scripture must be held in the highest regard, we must not neglect the power of story.

THE WHOLE STORY

The church is a part of God's story, but our chapter is not meant to be read from beginning to end. To live out the chapters intended for us, we must begin with the end in mind. The story is that God will not be stopped and history will not come to a close until the church accomplishes Jesus' purpose of redeeming people from every tribe and nation. Our chapter of the story only makes sense when we tell the whole story. There are many subplots in this great story: lives are changed, marriages are healed, relationships are restored, broken hearts are healed, and shattered dreams are reborn. But it all happens in the context of God calling us out to become fishers of men and conquerors of nations.

Other great stories are equally significant in the shaping of ethos. These stories are the stories of those within the culture whose names have faces and who not only bring the mythology of heroes and legends, but demonstrate the humanity of everyday people who are neighbors, family, and friends. First of all, there are stories that shape the leader and stories that develop deep within core beliefs and values that result in unwavering conviction, even in the face of disaster or conflict. Every leader has to stand in his story—the story of God in his life. And in that story, there may be many stories that explain an intimate knowledge of God. If people do not believe a leader has a true story of God, no other stories he tells will have a meaningful impact. You can remember the stories that have shaped your life—the stories that people tease you about because you tell them over and over again. These stories are more than a memory; they explain who you are and why you are going in the direction you're headed. They're stories of prayers answered, of obstacles overcome, of dreams fulfilled, and of sacrifices that realized the miraculous.

Apostolic leaders are not only great storytellers; in many ways their lives tell a great story. The stories we have lived only inspire us to call others to a similar journey, that they too may have their own stories of God.

Paul describes Christians as epistles, or letters of God, written on human hearts. With each story lived, the church becomes a place that is rich with God's stories; and with each story, faith increases and deepens. What then happens is that those without similar stories begin to search for their stories. They begin where those who have traveled their journey recommend they start. The Christian experience becomes a journey of discovery and experience with God, and with each added story, the momentum of this life-transforming movement exponentially increases.

WHEN A STORY COMES TO LIFE

One of the arts that leaders must craft is the selection of great stories. If all your stories come from outside your local culture, you'll end up with a diluted result. Almost nothing is more powerful than telling a story of transformation and then pointing to the person whose story it is, especially when everyone knows the person. One thing that is even more powerful is having him or her stand up and tell his or her own story.

Stories contain within them the essence of ethos. You can either talk to people about God's power or tell them the stories that unwrap the power of God. You can talk to them about the power of a small group community in the work of evangelism, or you can tell them a story that fleshes it out. You can tell people that creativity is not only the natural result of spirituality, but also an extraordinary tool for evangelism in the post-Western environment; or you can let them be the product of that reality. You can talk all day long about the importance of servanthood and service; or you can work from the pattern of Jesus and exalt those who humble themselves, giving positions of greatness to those who are willing to be the least in the kingdom. The stories you choose to tell inform the emerging culture. Stories that are rooted in the life of the congregation breathe life into the congregation. Great leaders are great storytellers. Great churches have great stories. Great stories create a great future.

YOUR WORDS DEFINE YOU

Another significant way that ethos is culturally transmitted is through language. Language is an important transmitter of culture, not only because it helps you describe your experience, but also because it helps you gain tools to survive and thrive in your particular environment. The same is true in the church environment. The more words you have for something, the more likely it is a genuine part of your ethos.

If you did a brief study of your cultural dictionary, what would emerge? How many words for evangelism would you have? How many words for servanthood? How many different ways of expressing and defining love? Do words like *risk*, *sacrifice*, *catalyze*, *innovate*, *create*, and *fail* surround the language of faith? Remember that the more nuanced the description, the more dominant the experience is in the culture. How many adjectives surround the word *love* in your context or illustrate the importance of hope in your community?

There is a difference between language that describes ethos and jargon or cliché. Jargon is the use of superficial and even meaningless language in an attempt to describe something that is more profound and substantive. It should concern us if we never move beyond the Christian language found on bumper stickers and T-shirts.

In the transmission of an ethos, it is essential that people can describe the genuineness of their own experience in their own words. For this reason, the language a leader chooses to use has tremendous impact on the shaping of a culture. At the same time, the ability of members of the community to clearly articulate and explain their values as their own is an essential evidence that an ethos is genuinely emerging.

RECLAIMING LANGUAGE

The meaning contained in the words we use is more significant than the words themselves. Two churches can use the same words and have dramatically different meanings. Every church uses the language of faith, love, and hope, but the meaning can be dramatically different. Every church uses some kind of language around servanthood and ministry, but the meaning won't be the same everywhere. To examine the power of language to shape ethos, we must go beyond the words that are spoken and evaluate honestly the meaning behind those words.

What does *fellowship* mean in your church? I have yet to meet a dying congregation that does not describe itself as having a great fellowship.

YOU CAN TALK ALL DAY LONG ABOUT THE IMPORTANCE OF SERVANTHOOD AND SERVICE; OR YOU CAN WORK FROM THE PATTERN OF JESUS AND EXALT THOSE WHO HUMBLE THEMSELVES, GIVING POSITIONS OF GREATNESS TO THOSE WHO ARE WILLING TO BE THE LEAST IN THE KINGDOM.

What does your church mean when it uses the word *missions*? It has always astonished me that so many churches and individuals who are "missions minded" rarely engage in the mission of Christ that requires them to come face to face with an unbeliever and love that person into God's kingdom.

There may be no more important word for us to evaluate in this area than the word *church*. What does it mean to be the church of Jesus Christ? What is an acceptable definition of a local church? When does a local church cease to be a church of Jesus Christ?

THE LEADER'S PRIMARY ROLE

The leader's primary role will be to nurture and awaken the apostolic ethos that sleeps within the heart of the church. At other times that calling will go beyond this metaphor, and the leader will be best described as a warrior-poet leading God's people to overtake the kingdom of darkness. Such a leader will deliver people from captivity into the freedom of Christ and will expand the kingdom of God, while creating the context from which new stories and songs are written.

Within all of these metaphors, the role of the pastor is inescapably one of spiritual leadership. If leadership is creating and shaping ethos, then spiritual leadership is creating and shaping an apostolic ethos within the local church. **C**

Used with permission from An Unstoppable Force: Daring to Become the Church God Had in Mind, *by Erwin Raphael McManus, published by Group Publishing, Inc. PO Box 481, Loveland, CO 80539,* **www.group.com.**

Erwin Raphael McManus is the Founding and Teaching Pastor for MOSAIC—a remarkably diverse ethnic and cultural congregation in Los Angeles. He is a national and international strategist and speaker on cultural, change, creativity and leadership. A consummate author, his other books include *Uprising*, and the *Barbarian Way*, and most recently *Chasing Daylight*. Learn more about Erwin at **www.mosaic.com.**

FUEL FOR THOUGHT
Use these questions to start a conversation on *Ethos* in your community.

1. *What metaphors contain the ethos of our congregation?*

2. *Is our church more like a crowd than a community? How can we move our group into deeper community?*

3. *Are we educating or catalyzing? Are we pulling or pushing? Is there movement?*

4. *Have a "telling": Share some of the great stories of your people.*

5. *What is your personal story? When have you seen God at work powerfully in your life?*

6. *How often do you share your stories?*

Book Review

"His moody, meandering style is pitch-perfect young Rose-City-bohemian prose."
— The Willamette Weekly (Portland, Oregon)

"A reminder that life was meant to be lived, not just gotten through."
— Publishers Weekly

DONALD MILLER
AUTHOR OF BLUE LIKE JAZZ

LIGHT, GOD, AND BEAUTY ON THE **OPEN ROAD**

THROUGH PAINTED DESERTS

TITLE:
Through Painted Deserts
AUTHOR: Donald Miller

REVIEW BY:
Michael Auliso

Having just ended a serious relationship, living in a new city far from home, and switching careers, I was in just the right mood to read a story of a young man's journey to find himself and a deeper meaning of life.

Through Painted Deserts by Donald Miller, author of the bestseller and critically acclaimed *Blue Like Jazz*, had me traveling vicariously with him and his friend Paul on their trek from Houston to Portland. I was immediately hooked from the first sarcastic interaction between the two, as it transported me back to numerous road trips with my own best friend—mile after mile of deep conversations, mindless banter, and wondering how soon we'd run out of money. The manner in which Miller jumps from a deep reflection on life to an astute observation of the mundane reminded me of my own schizophrenic thought process and drew me deeper into the tale of these two guys.

In addition to providing a breathtaking description of parts of the West, Miller also tackles many topics that truly resonate with me. As should be expected from two single guys, much of the focus was on girls. Is "the one" someone who provides you with stuff or just provides you with security? Are we really looking for "the one" or just some validation that comes from having someone on our arm? The straight-forward manner in which these issues are tackled made me realize that maybe I just need to relax and adopt the worry-free approach of these road warriors.

Finally, I was incredibly drawn to Don's views on life in general. We spend so much time working ourselves to the bone to acquire material possessions or accolades that fade moments later. Granted, not everyone can live a completely transient existence (and Don and Paul do reach their destination), but *Through Painted Deserts* forces you to realize that God has created a big world that we are meant to explore. We were intended to live our lives fully engaged rather than holed up in our homes, cities, and offices. This is a great tool to equip people of my generation as they reluctantly enter "the real world" without totally selling out. **C**

TRUE STORY

JASON MALEC

Experience Community

Jason Malec is experiencing life the way God designed us to experience it—in community with others. His journey there, however, was not a natural one.

Raised in a strict Roman Catholic family, college-bound Jason jettisoned his faith for a few years before slowly returning to Christ, and then enrolled at Gordon-Conwell Theological Seminary just weeks after marrying his wife Meredith. While there, ironically, he nearly fell away from his faith again. "Newly armed with tools to perform historical and reductive criticism—not to mention a healthy dose of pride—I questioned whether my faith and that of others was just a crutch to get us through life," Jason said. But through Meredith's patience and the support of a few good friends, he rediscovered a rich and vibrant faith.

No doubt Jason's past questioning of his faith gave him a unique compassion for those outside the faith asking questions about Spirituality. God used this past history to lead Jason to assist in the formation of The Portico, a Christian study community near Athens, Georgia, based on Francis and Edith Schaeffer's L'Abri. (**www.theportico.org**) Jason says, "I am committed to walking with people who have questions about Christianity." Participants live at The Portico for any length of time and participate in community—working, studying, eating and living together. During their stay, they meet regularly with tutors who monitor and shepherd their specialized study plan.

Jason's desire to influence his culture's perception of faith spills over to his other role—that of directing Starting Point, a conversational small group environment at North Point Community Church in a northern suburb of Atlanta. These 10-week short-term small groups give people—typically half of whom are unchurched—a taste of community. "Community is a place where we can know and be known, love and be loved, serve and be served, encourage and be encouraged," says Jason. "In simplest form, community is turning toward another. It is getting outside myself and intentionally getting inside someone else's world."

Jason sometimes compares life to a treadmill, one on which most of us are walking or running, while staring at whatever passing images show up on the monitor in front of us. "Those who have the courage to step off and take a look around," Jason says, "experience the richness, beauty and unpredictability of the world. Life without community is lonely and bland—black and white." For Jason, though, living in community with others is a life full of color. **C**

TRUE STORY

KRIS CHEEK

The Community of Sports

Kris Cheek is helping churches tap into a significant chunk of their communities—fans with a passion for sports. Through the mobile sports ministry of SportReach, an international sports organization founded and directed by Kris, churches are able to catch the vision of sports evangelism right in their own back-yards. (**www.sportreach.org**)

SportReach teams up with local churches to provide three-to-five-day athletic camps, focusing on high quality sports instruction and spiritual emphasis for children in third to sixth grades. They also reach out to teens in a 4-day event that revolves around extreme sports: skateboarding, rock climbing and BMX riding. Through demos, clinics, and competitions, SportReach is communicating the message: "The total athlete is complete in mind, body, and soul."

The son of a Bible camp director, Kris himself was immersed in the realm of sports from early age, and participated competitively through his college years. In 2001, Kris began to pursue his vision of full-time sports ministry. "Today across America and around the world," he says, "local churches are seeking avenues into a culture that is searching desperately for satisfaction and purpose." Many churches are beginning to use the mobile sports ministry as one avenue to tap into that un-reached culture.

Not bound by United States borders, SportReach also serves as an evangelistic platform worldwide, organizing sports mission trips to locations such as Lima, Peru. Partnership with missionaries and churches abroad has yielded numerous commitments to follow Christ, building connectivity and relationships between unreached families and the local church. Kris tells of a church-planting pastor in Lima, Juan Barrientos, who is excited about their partnership. "Juan estimates that 75 households—families that have had little interest in visiting the church—have been plugged into the local church ministry through the SportReach joint venture," Kris says.

Though his sights may be focused at times on the international scene, Kris still maintains a proper balance in his life. His personal journey with the Lord and dependence on the Holy Spirit is evident to those around him, especially a handful of young men he disciples every Tuesday morning—men with whom he walks "shoulder to shoulder." Kris yearns for others to catch the vision of reaching their culture with the gospel. "I want God to reproduce in others this hunger and restlessness He has placed in my spirit." **C**

TRUE STORY

KRISTIN ROGERS

It's Who You Know:
The Importance of Mentors
in the Life of a Leader

According to Kristin Rogers, it's who you know that determines what you become. Not because of their status or connections, but because she owes her success to the people who have inspired her along the way. And although Kristin has only just begun her life's journey, at the age of 24 she's already a national leadership consultant and business owner.

Raised by a single mother who supported the family as a Mary Kay cosmetics consultant, Kristin grew up watching her mother very closely. "The way that my mother strategically improved herself played a key role in my personal development. As she was emulating others, I was emulating her."

From her mother's example, Kristin learned the importance of committing to her goals early on. "Many people laughed when I told them my dream [to work for John Maxwell] and discouraged me from pursuing it, but I knew that if I stayed focused and was willing to step out on faith, God would create a path." Soon after college, Kristin landed her dream job and started tailoring leadership resources to people in the direct sales industry, like Mary Kay.

Surrounded by Christian leaders, Kristin was soon challenged to leave her comfort zone and take another step out on faith. Now, through her own business, Growing Up Pink™, Rogers travels around the nation sharing her story and providing women with leadership training and tips on how to involve their children in their home based business. (**www.growinguppink.com**)

Kristin attributes the greater part of her success to her mentors. "I know that if I hadn't actively sought out the role models and teachers that I did, I wouldn't be anywhere close to where I am today." She makes it a priority to know influential people on a personal level. "By surrounding myself with people who I admire, I have been able to closely observe them. I see how they approach and deal with situations, pray, and allow God to lead them."

Kristin, however, does not see herself as having crossed the finish line. "I will never stop growing. Everyday I am actively seeking out the next person with whom God has planned for me to cross paths." Obviously, Rogers considers growing up pink a lifelong process. **C**

YOUR STORY

From the beginning, we were designed to live in Community. It is an essential for young leaders to grow together, learn from others, and share in experiences. Are you intentional about community? What defines your "ethos"? Who is in your "inner-circle", serving as friends and mentors? Who are you pouring your life into? Tell the story of your community.

DYING

IN

THE

DESERT

OF

SELF

WE ARE LONELY PEOPLE, THOSE OF US WHO LIVE IN THE MARGINS. INSIDE EACH OF US IS THE LONGING TO BELONG, BUT WE FIND IT HARD TO ENGAGE IN THOSE RELATIONSHIPS THAT COULD BRING US INTO COMMUNITY. WE DON'T NECESSARILY HAVE THE RELATIONAL TOOLS TO ENTER INTO AUTHENTIC COMMUNITY, EVEN IF WE COULD FIND PEOPLE WHO WOULD ACCEPT US FOR WHO WE ARE.

By Rick McKinley

We come by it rightly, this need to be in relationship. When God created the first man, Adam, he said it was not good for the man to be alone. So he created Eve to be the man's wife. The first marriage gives us insight into human composition: We all need to belong.

Today we see people connected in all kinds of ways, all stemming from the longing to belong. Our world is getting smaller. Most of us can know what is going on anywhere else in the world at a moment's notice. We can communicate almost instantaneously via phone and e-mail with people in the most remote countries. The movies and TV shows that are popular in America soon become popular around the globe.

I have two good friends who grew up in Ireland. I was visiting there for a few weeks when we first met. While talking we soon realized that we shared many of the same interests. We had grown up watching the same movies. They knew where Yellowstone National Park was because of Yogi Bear (who lived in the fictional Jellystone). We sang U2 songs together. We discovered that we spoke a common language—the language of popular culture.

Of course, I probably had the same things in common with many other Irish people. But there was something more that connected the three of us, something that would make us good friends,

lasting friends. There was a bigger story that ran through all three of our lives: the Christ story.

We had Christ in common.

Our common experience of his love and grace is the thing that has kept our hearts knit together. Culture could not take us there. Culture gave us affinity; Christ gave us a common unity. We were all three united in Christ.

The fact is, culture cannot offer us real community. It offers us entertainment. It offers us material things. But it can't offer us what we deeply long for—relationship. Even though billions of people are connected by common points of cultural reference, there is still tremendous loneliness. We spend our lives in chat rooms with made-up names and tell people things about ourselves that are not true. We find a sense of shared identity in a favorite sports team or a musician that we both like. That is not community; it is affinity. We climb into our beds at night insecure because no one really knows us. We don't usually lie there awake, going over it in our minds. No, it's more like static, white noise in the back of our hearts. It's always buzzing at us, but we tune it out.

What about the church? Can't we find community there? The relationship Jesus has brought us into with the Father is supposed to overflow into our relationships with one another.

We're supposed to be a family. Brothers and sisters in Christ.

Tragically, for most of us the church is not a place where we feel we can be authentic. After all, what if somebody there should find out that I'm struggling with sin, that I'm not living the victorious Christian life? So we all put on masks and cover up what's really going on. And our sin grows in isolation.

Isolation is the garden of the devil. If he can convince you not to be real with people and shame you into thinking that you're the only one who thinks like that or has failed, he can get you off to the sidelines and keep you there. Your heart will begin to shrivel up and your faith will be deeply challenged. That is why the margins are so prevalent in the church. Somewhere along the line we bought into the world's understanding of how we're supposed to do life. We started keeping up appearances, and in that place we were robbed of the communal faith that Jesus died to give us.

You and I were never called to live this Christian life alone. Community is central to being a Christ follower, and it's vital to reimagining life in Jesus. Satan can have his way with believers as long as they're stuck in the margins, and so he has taught us to believe any number of lies.

THE LIE OF INDIVIDUALISM

The lie of individualism is a huge lie we've bought into here in America. This began a few hundred years ago with the onset of modernity. It essentially says that all understanding begins with me—I am the center of my universe. I can make something of myself. I can be a self-made person. I will win. When the world is implicitly about me then it cannot be about you, at least not in my thinking.

This lie flies in the face of Christ's example. Consider Peter, a businessman. Here's a guy who has made it. He has the house, the car, the wife, and the cash. But he is still lonely. Why? Because he is stuck in the margins of individualism. He believes that he's traveling on a one lane road and the most important use of his resources is to fill his lane with whatever makes him happy.

The path of individualism breeds a self-centeredness that we cannot shake. Even in our best deeds, we still look for the payoff to us.

WHAT'S IN IT FOR ME?

The culture we live in is about our making it for our glory. Plain and simple. The result of this is that people fail to engage in deep relationships. There are few places where they are really known, not even in their own marriages and families. Everyone is too busy looking out for themselves.

This same individualism has crept into the church with tragic results. These days we like to say that our faith is "a private matter." It's just about me and Jesus. Get out of my lane. This has created a church culture that personalizes faith to the detriment of community. We've bought into the lie that if we're to connect people to God we must first meet their individualistic needs. On Sunday when a family arrives at church, we send their kids off to age-specific classes, while the wife goes to a class for women her age and the husband attends a class for men. When they get back to the car they seldom talk about what they experienced. Why? Because there is an unspoken rule: This is my lane and you don't get to tell me what to do or believe. Worry about your own lane. Mine is fine.

By segmenting everyone into age-specific classes or special interest groups, we reinforce the lie of individualism. We implicitly teach that the church is there to meet the individual's needs. We treat them like spectators in the process, not key participants. This approach puts the church in the position of selling Jesus—trying to get you to come by catering to your specific needs.

If faith is truly a private matter, then the only thing Christians have in common is a regular event called church, and there is no authentic relationship with one another in Christ. The shame of spiritual isolation is compounded when we realize that even at church no one knows who we really are. I talked with one person who told me that if anyone at church really knew who she was, the doubts and struggles she faced, they simply would not accept her. That floats over her head like a cartoon thought-bubble in a comic strip. It forces her to smile at church and tell everyone how great she is doing. The irony is, everyone there has the same bubble over their head and is thinking the same thing. And our enemy Satan has a field day.

Jesus and the New Testament writers tell us that we need each other. We need each other to help us develop into all that God intends for us to become. In Galatians 5:13, we are told to use the freedom that Christ purchased for us not to keep sinning and abuse his grace, but to serve one another. You and I now exist for other people. We are to shift our focus away from ourselves and onto others, to look for ways to love and take care of other people.

Christ set us free so we could leave our lanes and look out for one other.

People in prison have to look out for themselves. There, selfishness is at the very core of survival. Fights break out over food and cigarettes, because inmates have nothing and must take what they can for themselves. But we are not in prison; we have been set free by Jesus. So why do we insist on using our freedom for self-gain and not to help others?

In the world's economy, life is not much different from prison—we're all fighting to get what we can out of life. But the church is not supposed to mimic our culture or the life of those who are not free. Instead, it is meant to be a place where people are so grateful that Jesus has given his life for their sin that they are looking for a chance to mimic him by serving others. We are to serve one another and complement one another's gifts for the common purpose of representing Christ to our world.

Jesus invites you to reimagine life as a key participant in his family. The ball is in your court.

THE LIE OF AUTONOMY

The crippling lie of self-sufficiency led to the first sin, when Satan convinced Adam and Eve that they didn't need God. This lie has since been woven into the fabric of our culture and the church: I don't need anyone to tell me what to do. I can take care of myself. I am perfectly capable of making my own decisions. And so we strive for autonomy, for independence, but when a person finally achieves it he dies inside. That's because we were never meant to take care of ourselves. Each of us was created to be dependent—on God and on one another.

We are wired for community. Literally. Each of us has a belly button. Some are outies, some are innies, some are pierced. But we all carry this unmistakable sign that shows we were at one time physically connected to our mothers. Life begins for every human in utter dependence on another. But as we grow, our culture slowly sucks us into believing that we will truly be liberated only when we no longer need to depend on someone else. Yet in our liberation we find oppression—we fight for autonomy only to end up lonely, tired, and struggling.

We've all met someone who is difficult to work with. You know the type: It's either my way or the highway. You can't get very far with these people. They're autonomous. But self-sufficiency is also more subtle than that. It creeps into our way of thinking. We pass judgment on others who are not like us. We find it hard to trust God and almost impossible to trust other people. We are reluctant to expose our true selves, our thoughts, our emotions. We hold our cards close to the vest. We try to be our own god, and we wear ourselves out trying to control our own universe. And all the time we still have the need to belong. So we try to fill our longing with sin and end up more broken than when we started.

WE ARE WIRED FOR COMMUNITY

Some of us try to belong and be autonomous at the same time, but it doesn't work. You often see this in the church. If we don't like what the pastor says, we fire him. If we don't like the music, we complain. If the leadership tries to corral us into a small group, we buck even harder. Finally, if our needs aren't being catered to, we leave. We take our money with us and think, "That'll teach them."

Jesus wants us to reimagine ourselves as participants in his redeemed family. Note that I say participant, not spectator. But the lie of autonomy tells us that the lack of love in the church is someone else's problem, not mine.

So we sit in the bleachers and watch.

We watch as people are hurting and need a friend. We sit idly by as our leaders try to move people toward community. It's not my problem that I'm self-sufficient, we think. Jesus says that's a lie. We belong to one another because we belong to Christ. We need to come down out of the stands and do something for someone.

THE LIE OF AFFINITY
We tend to gravitate to people who are like us. People who look like us, talk like us, make about the same money we do, believe what we believe, and enjoy the same entertainment we do. Is that community? No, that's affinity. We're alike so we can be friends. What this really boils down to is self-worship. I like you because you are like me. We share the same tastes. I can hang out with you. We are essentially surrounding ourselves with ourselves, only with different names and faces. We may develop a circle of acquaintances this way, but we won't experience the deeper things that make belonging in community the beautiful, biblical thing that it is.

Tragically, the church has bought into the culture's lie of affinity. We go to churches that are full of people just like us. We don't go to this church because Jesus has redeemed us to belong to one another; we go to this church because the members all belong to the same ethnicity or we listen to the same music or we vote the same way or all of the above. We go to this church because the people are just like us. It doesn't take an act of God to get people to like each other if they are all alike. You can find that in any subculture in America.

To the world, the church looks like just another subculture.

In Ephesians 4:2, the author tells us to be humble and gentle, to be patient, bearing with one another in love. We are called to be humble because, before God, that guy who bugs you is on the same plane you are. You both needed Christ to die for you. Jesus doesn't see you as a peer and the other guy as a loser. Jesus invites us to humble ourselves from that pride, to bear with one another in love. I sometimes wish he would have said "tolerate." I can do that. I can put up with someone. That's not what the Bible says, though. The command to bear with one another in love assumes that people are going to bug you. This is where the lie of affinity makes it tough.

We're willing to travel next to people driving in their own lanes as long as they are kind of like us. But put me next to people who are nothing like me and I want to steer away from them. Jesus tells me that's destructive to his family. He wants me to get my eyes off myself and onto others and bear with them in love. I need to get to know them beyond their annoying habits and see their heart. Caring for people who are different from me is not the pastor's job or the small-group leader's job. It is my job and your job and we need to do it out of love. That pulls us out of the margins of affinity and into the heart of God's family.

In John 14, Jesus tells us to love one another as he has loved us. If God's family really took this seriously and loved one another as Jesus has loved us, we would see a group of people who forgive each other, people who are devoted to each other, people who respect and care for one another. This would be a family of people who don't judge one another but, rather, encourage one another to live life as Jesus has defined it for us. That kind of love looks really strange in this world. In the same passage, Jesus says that all people will know we are his disciples by our love for one another. In other words, his brand of love is so utterly foreign to this me-first world that people will know you are following Christ if you love like that.

The question is simple. Does the love you have for God's family look like the love Jesus has for you? You are a participant. No one is off the hook. When

you reimagine yourself as a key player in God's family, you choose to love others instead of waiting for them to love you. You are walking in the messy blessing of community.

THE MESSY BLESSING OF COMMUNITY
The picture of the church in the Bible is a messy one. Why? Because community is messy. The lies our culture wants us to buy into are not new. The church has struggled against them since its birth. The mess happens when people who are not like each other begin to do life together. We soon realize that community requires us to fall at Jesus' feet and beg him for the love it takes to obey the "one another" commands. We find we often have to ask people to forgive us because we have not served and loved them the way Jesus wanted us to.

Imagine you're in a group of people getting together to worship. You are all pretty similar. Then a couple of other Christ-followers walk in. One has come straight out of rehab. He's been strung out on drugs for several years and has just given his life to Jesus. The other guy is a wealthy businessman who has just sold his company for fifty million dollars. How do you suppose your group will respond to these two very different men? Will you kiss up to the guy with cash and try to be polite to the guy who just got off drugs? Or will you avoid the guy with cash (because he probably thinks he's better than you) and cater to the guy who is out of rehab (because you think you're better than him and, therefore, he is safe)? Do you question the one guy's motives and wonder if he will really stay sober? Are you so enamored with the rich guy's lifestyle that you're ready to make him a small-group leader?

Why are we like this? It's because we believe the cultural values our world has taught us and we're reluctant to submit to the messy community that Christ has called us into.

Now imagine that Jesus is in the room.

How does he see these men? Jesus knows that they both needed his grace and that he had to die to redeem both of them. Therefore, they are both deserving of surpassing love and devotion from other believers. You need them. They need you. They even need each other. Behind the tattoos and the business suit is the same

THEN WE MUST REIMAGINE LIFE, PICTURING THIS NEW REALITY OF PARTICIPATING IN AUTHENTIC COMMUNITY. WE EXIST FOR GOD AND OTHERS. LET THAT BE THE MOTTO OF OUR LIVES. LET'S NOT WAIT FOR SOMEONE ELSE TO OBEY JESUS.

kind of broken life. That's the great thing about authentic community. It's the real us in loving relationship with other real people, all under the grace of the real and living Christ.

So how do we enter into this messy blessing of community? First, we need to believe that what Jesus says is true. Then we need to quit buying into the individualistic lies of our culture. We need to admit to God that we have been living under the power of these lies and, therefore, have not been living in biblical community.

Then we must reimagine life, picturing this new reality of participating in authentic community. We exist for God and others. Let that be the motto of our lives. Let's not wait for someone else to obey

Jesus. Be courageous. Find someone who is not like you—perhaps someone older or younger, richer or poorer—and ask that person to meet with you once a week to talk about life and faith and what Jesus is doing in their life and yours. Be honest with one another. Share your mistakes.

Confess your sins to one another. The Bible says this will be a healing time.

You will find that Jesus is in the midst of that kind of community. Will you leave your one-lane life to love your brothers and sisters? **C**

Excerpted from Jesus in the Margins © *2005 by Rick McKinley. Used by permission of Multnomah Publishers, Inc.*

Rick McKinley is the lead pastor at Imago Dei Community Church in Portland, Oregon. **(www.imagodeicommunity.com)**.

53 YEARS iN SPACE

BY DONALD MILLER

ONE OF MY HOUSEMATES, STACY, ASKED ME TO WRITE A STORY ABOUT AN ASTRONAUT. IN HIS STORY THE ASTRONAUT IS WEARING A SUIT THAT KEEPS HIM ALIVE BY RECYCLING HIS FLUIDS. IN THE STORY THE ASTRONAUT IS WORKING ON A SPACE STATION WHEN AN ACCIDENT TAKES PLACE, AND HE IS CAST INTO SPACE TO ORBIT THE EARTH, TO SPEND THE REST OF HIS LIFE CIRCLING THE GLOBE.

Stacy says this story is how he imagines hell, a place where a person is completely alone, without others and without God. After Stacy told me about his story, I kept seeing it in my mind. I thought about it before I went to sleep at night. I imagined myself looking out my little bubble helmet at blue earth, reaching towards it, closing it between my puffy white space-suit fingers, wondering if my friends were still there. In my imagination I would call out to them, yell for them, but the sound would only come back loud within my helmet. Through the years my hair would grow long in my helmet and gather around my forehead and touch my face with my hands to move my hair out of my eyes, so

my view of earth, slowly, over the first two years, would dim to only a thin light through a curtain of thatch and beard.

I would lay there in bed thinking about Stacy's story, putting myself out there in the black. And there came a time, in space, when I could not tell whether I was awake or asleep. All my thoughts mingled together because I had no people to remind me what was real and what was not real. I would punch myself in the side to feel pain, and this way I could be relatively sure I was not dreaming. Within ten years I was beginning to breathe heavy through my hair and my beard as they were pressing tough against my face and begun to

curl into my mouth and up my nose. In space, I forgot that I was human. I did not know whether I was a ghost or an apparition or a demon thing.

After I thought about Stacy's story, I lay there in bed and wanted to be touched, wanted to be talked to. I had the terrifying thought that something like that might happen to me. I thought it was just a terrible story, a painful and ugly story. Stacy had delivered as accurate a description of hell as could be calculated. And what is sad, what is very sad, is that we are proud people, and because we have sensitive egos and so many of us live our lives in front of our televisions, not having to deal with real people who might

hurt us or offend us, we float along on our couches like astronauts moving aimlessly through the Milky Way, hardly interacting with other humans beings at all.

Stacy's story frightened me so badly I called my friend Penny. Penny is who I call when I'm thinking too much. She knows this sort of thing. It was late, but I asked her if I could come over. She said yes. I took the bus from Laurelhurst, and there were only a few people on the bus, and none of them were talking to each other. When I got to Reed, Penny greeted me with a hug and a kiss on the cheek. We hung out in her room for a while and made small talk. It was so nice to hear another human voice. She had a picture of her father on her desk, tall and thin and wearing a cowboy hat. She told me about her father and how, when she was a child, she and her sister Posie spent a year sailing in the Pacific. She said they were very close. I listened so hard because I felt like, while she was telling

LONELINESS IS SOMETHING THAT HAPPENS TO US, BUT I THINK IT IS SOMETHING WE CAN MOVE OURSELVES OUT OF. I THINK A PERSON WHO IS LONELY SHOULD DIG INTO A COMMUNITY, GIVE HIMSELF TO A COMMUNITY, HUMBLE HIMSELF BEFORE HIS FRIENDS, INITIATE COMMUNITY, TEACH PEOPLE TO CARE FOR EACH OTHER, LOVE EACH OTHER.

me stories, she was massaging my soul, letting me know I was not alone, that I will never have to be alone, that there are friends and family and churches and coffee shops. I was not going to be cast into space.

Loneliness is something that happens to us, but I think it is something we can move ourselves out of. I think a person who is lonely should dig into a community, give himself to a community, humble himself before his friends, initiate community, teach people to care for each other, love each other. Jesus does not want us floating in space or sitting in front of our televisions. Jesus wants us interacting, eating together, laughing together, praying together. Loneliness is something that came with the fall. If loving other people is a bit of heaven, then certainly isolation is a bit of hell, and to that degree, here on earth, we decide in which state we would like to live. **C**

Adapted by permission of Thomas Nelson Inc., Nashville, TN, from the book entitled Blue Like Jazz, *copyright © 2003 by Donald Miller. All rights reserved.*

Donald Miller is the author of *Blue Like Jazz, Searching for God Knows What,* and the most recently *Through Painted Deserts.* In addition to these titles and articles written for numerous magazines, Don is a frequent speaker, focusing on the merit of Christian spirituality as an explanation for beauty, meaning, and the human struggle. For booking information, visit **www.BlueLikeJazz.com.**

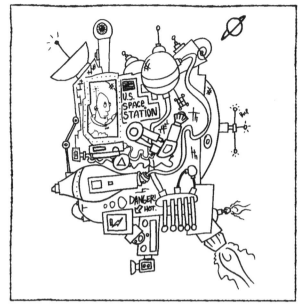

There once was a man named
Don Astronaut.

Don Astronaut lived on
a space station out in space.

DON THE ASTRONAUT

Don Astronaut had
a special space suit that kept
him alive without food or
water or oxygen.

One day there was an accident.

And Don Astronaut was
cast out into space.

Don Astronaut orbited the earth
and was very scared.

Until he remembered his special
suit that kept him alive.

But nobody's government came
to rescue Don Astronaut because
it would cost too much money.
(There was a conspiracy, and they
said he had died, but he hadn't.)

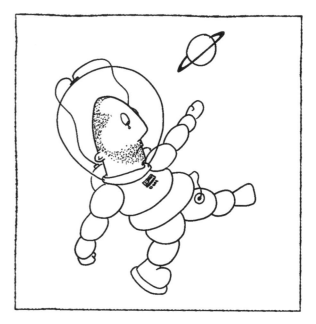

So Don Astronaut
orbited the earth again
and again, fourteen
times each day.

And Don Astronaut orbited
the earth for months.

And Don Astronaut orbited
the earth for decades.

And Don Astronaut orbited the earth
for fifty-three years before he died a
very lonely and crazy man—just a shell of
a thing with hardly a spark for a soul.

HOMELESS JOURNEY
GOD'S CALL STRENGTHENED THROUGH COMMUNITY

BY MIKE YANKOSKI

ABOUT MIDWAY THROUGH MY FRESHMAN YEAR OF COLLEGE, I FELT CALLED TO SOMETHING DIFFERENT THAN WHAT I'D ALWAYS KNOWN: HOMELESSNESS. I DON'T MEAN VOLUNTEERING AT A LOCAL SHELTER, BUT ACTUALLY TO THE HOMELESS LIFESTYLE. I FELT CALLED TO BE HOMELESS. NOT PERMANENTLY, BUT AT LEAST FOR A WHILE IN ORDER TO EXPERIENCE WHAT MILLIONS OF MEN AND WOMEN ACROSS THE STREETS OF THE UNITED STATES OF AMERICA DO EVERY DAY.

I had no idea where to even start. I began doing lots of research, reading books and biographies and sociological studies on the homeless problem. After nearly a year of inquiry, I felt pretty well-versed and informed. But there was a problem. About four months before I was to set out on the "Homeless Journey" I awoke at three a.m. in a cold sweat. I felt in my gut that something essential was missing from all my preparations. It hit me that in all of my research, planning and education had resulted in accurate and necessary information. But I was lacking something critical: wise counsel.

T.S. Eliot's question, "Where is the wisdom we have lost in knowledge? Where is the knowledge we have lost in information?" struck home. I had a lot of information, but no wisdom. Here I was, about to launch out into one of the biggest decisions I'd ever made. I felt called to it and knew that God was asking me to venture out in faith with Him. Yet I asked myself, "Why had I for so long been preparing alone?" I realized that by going solo I had been telling myself and everyone else that I could accomplish this on my own—I didn't need anybody else's insight, experience, and most sickeningly, anybody else's wisdom.

The Bible proclaims often that wisdom is wrapped up in the Lord Jesus Christ. If you want wisdom, then you need Him. "The fear of the Lord is the beginning of wisdom," says Proverbs 1:7 (NIV). If we want to act wisely, to live life with wisdom, and to actually become wise we must fear (that is, have reverence for, and stand humbly in the presence of) the Lord. Only from that place, that foundation and beginning, can we grow in wisdom. But there is also a human face to Godly wisdom which we can approach in our lives. Proverbs 11:14 states that "many advisers makes victory sure." (NIV) No matter how capable we may feel at something, no matter how informed we may assume ourselves to be, seeking other people's perspectives helps to fortify, build up and strengthen any endeavor. "There's nothing new under the sun," (Ecclesiastes 1:9 NIV) it is a promise that we can find someone who will be able to help us prepare and understand where are about to venture. There are people who

the best way to go. Through the collective experience and wisdom of my group of mentors and advisers, we changed the entire course of the journey. Because I asked these men to weigh in from different perspectives and positions, the calling I knew was from God actually became stronger and wiser.

Seeking wise council can certainly seem intimidating and at first. Asking for someone else's help often feels like we are admitting, "I can't do this!" or, "I'm incapable!" However, I realized an important truth through my own planning process: Asking for another's opinion and wisdom is really saying, "Although I could do this alone, it would be far better to get other's help and make sure I'm

to become the best husband that I can be and she wants become the best wife she can be. And guess what—we don't have any experience! Our older friends and counselors have asked us the hard questions. Through our conversations, the ideas and perspectives and wisdom they've offered have changed the way that both of us are approaching our marriage.

Recently I watched an epic war movie with some friends. Flashing swords, screaming arrows, valiant armies and virtuous pursuits filled my mind for a full two hours—and I loved every second of it. Of course it was a multi-million dollar creation of Hollywood that probably wasn't very historically accurate, but I really didn't care.

RESEARCH, PLANNING AND EDUCATION HAD RESULTED IN ACCURATE AND NECESSARY INFORMATION. BUT I WAS LACKING SOMETHING CRITICAL: WISE COUNSEL

have gone before us into a particular area or topic and have valuable insight. We, on the other hand, are less experienced and merely have ideas. When it comes to the really important questions, I would take someone's tried and true experience over even my best research every time.

The day after that three a.m. panic, I got to work recruiting wise counsel. I sought out those who had life experience, specifically older men of faith, starting with the local rescue mission president and a professor from my college. Over the next months, these men asked really difficult questions, talked through different ideas with me, made powerful suggestions, and prayed for me. Soon thereafter I asked six other men to join together and form an official board of advisers. Together, this group of eight men changed the course of the months I planned to live on the streets.

During my solo planning stages I had decided on six cites to live in while homeless. The board of advisers listened to my ideas about the cities, and then actually recommended changing five of the six. Initially I was shocked (and my ego damaged). After all of my independent research and planning, I hadn't chosen

going in the best direction." Choosing to seek wise council from others means that you care so much about your decision or action that you will do whatever it takes to move in the most equipped and educated direction possible.

My wife and I are newly weds. During our engagement period I became more aware of how weighty a covenant we are making together. We were committing to love and cherish one another and to sacrifice ourselves on the other's behalf. It is an exciting and an intimidating responsibility. To be married is a daily decision to die to self and trust that my needs will be taken care of even as I focus on serving my wife's needs before my own.

The week after she said "Yes" to the big question, we began meeting with several older marriage counselors in order to help us grow in wisdom about our life-changing decision. Of course we could have tried to make our engagement and marriage work without counsel and wisdom, and by God's grace we probably would have survived. But who wants to merely survive marriage? We want to thrive. We decided that our relationship is so important that we needed to do everything we could to strengthen ourselves. I want

In one of the last scenes, the powerful warrior stands in the center of an arena, enemies slain beside him, surrounded and revered by the cheering crowds, undeniably victorious. The moment is paramount and adrenaline surged through my body. Every bit of me ached to be the main character, wanting to stand as he does, at the center of it the world, unconquerable, loudly proclaiming, "Look what I have accomplished!" There's a part of all of us that wants others to know that we were able to achieve great things on our own.

But there's something horribly wrong in the scene.

The warrior is dying.

Going it alone has killed him.

Desiring everything that you undertake to succeed to the Glory of the Lord Jesus Christ means humbly realizing that you don't know everything, seeking wise council from others who have gone before you, and allowing people to help you in the journey.

Only a fool journeys alone. C

Mike Yankoski, a recent graduate of Westmont College, is the author of *Under the Overpass: A Journey of Faith on the Streets of America* (Mulnomah, 2005). He seeks to live out his faith with radical intensity, and intentionally pursues a lifestyle that reaches others for Christ and glorifies God. He and his wife, Danae, live in Santa Barbara, California. Find more information at (www.UnderTheOverpass.com).

MENTOR: Wanted

A MENTORING RELATIONSHIP WILL VARY BASED ON THE SCOPE AND NATURE OF YOUR NEEDS; HOWEVER, WHAT YOU LOOK FOR IN A MENTOR WILL NOT. POTENTIAL MENTORS ARE ALL AROUND YOU, IF YOU KNOW WHAT YOU'RE LOOKING FOR. THEY DON'T HAVE TO BE SPECTACULAR TALENTS OR EXTREMELY WEALTHY. MORE OFTEN THAN NOT, PEOPLE IN THAT CATEGORY ARE EITHER DELUGED WITH REQUESTS OR HAVE FULL SCHEDULES. WE PUT TOGETHER A SNAPSHOT OF A MENTOR TO GET YOU STARTED ON YOUR SEARCH.

Experience Desired

Your would-be-mentor (WBM) has to have something in his or her life you want in yours. This could take many forms: knowledge, experience, wisdom, etc. Do they have to be a genius? No! Mentoring is not rocket science. It is about the transfer – the passing on. Think of a group of elders sitting around the fire telling stories. These stories, experiences and insights go a long way. You can't shortcut life.

Must Be a Good Listener

You need someone who will listen to you. Depending on your needs, he or she may need to listen 80 to 90 percent of the time. The percentage is not the issue; it's the attitude and climate of the exchange. Are you really being heard? Is he or she answering the questions you asked? If not, then you don't have a mentor, you have a talking head. The stories may be great, but the benefit is a whopping zero. You can try and salvage the relationship. Better yet, avoid it in the first place.

Looking for Similar Interests

Do others already consult your WBM? Is he or she sought out by others for wisdom and advice? If so, great! You could have a mentor on the line. Do some more homework: What has he or she consulted about mostly? If it is addiction counseling and you are looking for a church planting sage or business entrepreneur, don't expect all those skills to be transferable. Even more specifically, what kind of ministry or business help do you need? A senior teaching pastor may know nothing about children's ministry programming. A Fortune 500 CEO may know nothing about launching a start-up on a shoestring budget. Don't settle. Keep Searching.

Strong Relational Skills

The essence of mentoring is a relationship. Does your WBM currently cultivate relationships with peers? Don't count on building something long-term and highly relational with a reclusive academic who has spent his or her life in research. At the same time, don't overlook them if you need to learn about current research methods. If your needs are more targeted and technical, you might not need a holistic mentoring relationship. Only you will know.

Connections are Preferred

How networked is your WBM? Mentors not only impart wisdom, but they also give you an inside track into the world that might otherwise be tough to crack. This isn't a license for shameless name dropping, but an advance call or reference letter from someone in the loop is worth its weight in plutonium. Again, they don't need to have an audience with the president to be able to help you out. Sometimes just knowing the best vendor in your region will save you hours of cold calling and could even get you better rates.

Positive Thinking and Encouragement Expected

Your WBM will have to take a chance on you. Unless you have known him or her for years, you will be asking someone to believe in you and to have the discernment to see latent potential within you. Don't be surprised if you get run through a fairly rigorous interview process on the front end of the relationship. Your WBM will need to see a spark of hope in you. A good Mentor won't take that lightly, and neither should you. **C**

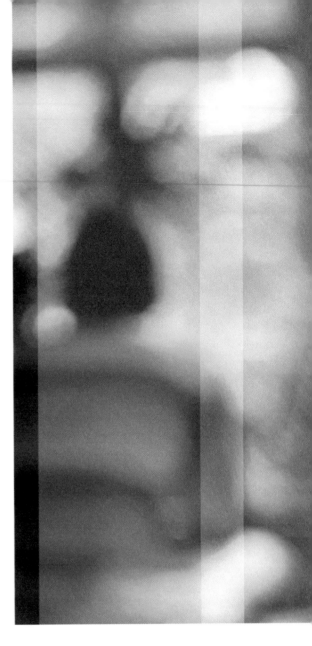

How to find a PROTÉGÉ

THERE IS A GENERATION OF YOUNG MEN AND WOMEN CLAMORING FOR THE ATTENTION OF SOMEONE WHO WILL GIVE A LITTLE TIME AND A LOT OF WISDOM. WHETHER YOU ARE A YOUTH PASTOR IN THE MIDST OF FIGURING OUT YOUR NEXT STEP, OR A MID-MANAGER LOOKING FOR A POTENTIAL STAR, OUR GUIDE TO THE PROTÉGÉ WILL HELP YOU SPOT THE DIAMONDS IN THE ROUGH.

Passion

The traditional model of mentoring is that someone a little further down the road helps those new to the trail. It is not a prerequisite, though. What is a prerequisite is hunger. Don't waste your time and experience on someone looking to coast through life. Is your would-be-protégé looking to grow and shoulder a bigger load? Great! You can deal with ambition and over-achieving. You could deal with laziness, too, but it's not your battle.

Vision

If they don't have a goal or a dream of who they desire to become, you don't have a protégé. This doesn't mean you cannot help to clarify goals. It does

mean the protégé cannot be goal-averse. You will hit what you aim at, even if it is nothing. If a protégé doesn't have a clear goal, walk him or her through a calling and purpose process and tell them to come back when they know. You cannot create and meet goals for them, no matter how much you desire.

Centered

Your protégé has to be comfortable with the fact that the responsibility is in him to "own" the results of the relationship. Does he or she accept personal responsibility for where they are in life—for both failures and successes? If not, don't waste your time. You will only be the next name on the list of people (or institutions) who have failed to help

them with their life's problems (primarily themselves). Again there are exceptions. Proceed with caution (and discernment).

Confidence

You can spend a lot of time divulging your experience to the human equivalent of a brick wall. Does he or she need to be brilliant? No. Is this about IQ? No. It is about being teachable and proactive. Do they ask questions? How do they respond to criticism? You will need to probe for proactivity. Make sure you thoroughly interview your protégé. You are about to invest learning's from your life into them. It is OK to scrutinize candidates. What have they read lately? What experience do they have? What have they learned in their current position? What have they learned

in the last week? This one characteristic could be the deciding factor between a successful or failed relationship.

Initiative

If you are approaching him or her, make sure they are self motivated and disciplined. If they approached you, how was the initial contact? Reticent and shy, or confident and sure? Don't overlook the smoldering flax in the first one. Self-confidence might be the best thing you can impart, but nothing will be like strapping a rocket booster onto the back of someone who has their eyes fixed on the prize. With you to point out the potholes and steer clear of the ditches, you and your new friend are in for a great journey. **C**

Journal

What does INTENTIONAL ABOUT COMMUNITY mean to me?

THINK

COURAGEOUS in Calling

Do I have the courage to act on what God has called me to do?

God has a unique purpose that He desires to carry out in me. To know this purpose I must first know Him. To fulfill this purpose, I must trust Him and have the courage to act on it, which may feel like a risk. My talents and heart converge to create my calling and purpose. I am competent in my calling because I am committed to further developing and honing my talents and skills. My foundational understanding of how God is working during my current season of life determines the specific way I apply this calling vocationally.

FINDING YOUR PURPOSE AND CALLING

Influence Explodes When You Know You Know

By Ben Ortlip

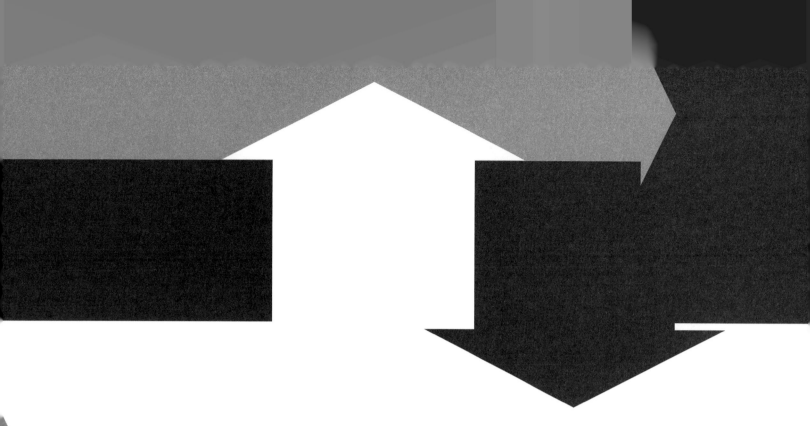

IT'S OFFICIAL. WE ARE NOW LIVING IN THE PURPOSE GENERATION. SOCIOLOGISTS COINED THE TERM "GEN-ERATION X" TO DESCRIBE OUR CULTURE'S IDENTITY CRISIS. NEXT CAME "GENERATION WHY?", SO NAMED FOR THE ABSENCE OF MEANING AND PURPOSE. AND NOW IT SEEMS WE ARE COMING FULL CIRCLE. THE CURRENT GENERATION WILL HERETOFORE BE KNOWN AS THE PURPOSE GENERATION ... OKAY, SO I'M THE ONLY ONE CALLING IT THAT SO FAR. BUT WHEN IT CATCHES ON, YOU HEARD IT HERE FIRST.

Regardless of what you call it, our nation is engaged in an all-out quest for answers.

Just ask Barnes and Noble. Sales of titles like *The DaVinci Code*, *The Celestine Prophecy*, and the *Purpose-Driven Life* have been dominating the cash registers for months. Name any five movies released by Hollywood in the last year and chances are three of them dealt with this theme, directly or indirectly. The word on the street is that we must be here for a reason, and the first person to come up with the answer wins a lifetime supply of happiness.

So what should church leaders be doing to maximize their influence during this incredible harvest season? Well, you already know "the answer" to the world's great search. So you've got that going for you. But chances are, your own sense of purpose and calling could use a little firming up. And that could have a big effect on your ability to impact this generation.

It has been suggested that one of the greatest contributors to the confusion of recent generations is the church's own lack of conviction. We're not talking about you, of course. But confidence in the church as a source of answers to life has definitely seen its ups and downs. As a result, church leaders need more than just the mark of the clergy if they want to be recognized as a guidepost for answers to a searching world. If you really want to be influential, there needs to be something on the inside that distinguishes you as a sentinel of certainty. And what better than a strong sense of your own purpose and calling?

Got Mojo?

Certainty is a rare commodity in our culture. And yet, certainty is the single most influential quality a person can possess. The world calls it confidence. Austin Powers calls it "Mojo." Whatever your name for it, there's something about a person who just knows they've got it. And when it comes to influence, there's nothing so influential as the assurance of one's purpose. The world is desperate to know that it's possible to believe in something so strongly that you're willing to live for it ... or even die for it. When they

see someone with that kind of conviction, it's magnetic. They can't help being influenced by it. Influence explodes when you know you know.

Frankly, this quality is lacking in the church today. Sure, we've got the assurance of salvation. But when it comes to brandishing a sense of destiny in God's universe, we've lost our mojo. It's one thing to know what the world needs. But it's another to know that you're on a specific mission to deliver it. That's when confidence translates into a set of convictions, and ideals turn into ideas. That's what it means to know your purpose and calling.

In Scripture, it's pretty clear that God has specific plans in mind for every soul on the planet. It's not like you have to be an Archbishop to be worthy of God's attention and forethought. Each of us has unique gifts and his own set of fingerprints to leave on the world. As Ephesians 2:10 describes, God has been preparing in advance for the events in your life. And each of us has an assignment to live out during our lifetime.

Nevertheless, very few Christians have the gumption to take a shot at figuring out what it is. At least, not with much certainty and specificity. But unfortunately, you'll never reach your maximum influence until you develop convictions about your purpose in life. You'll never find your mojo until you're ready to take bold, written steps toward a life of certainty about your unique calling.

Hellenist or Hebrew?

Perhaps it will help to look at why we resist in the first place. You can trace it all back to the classic western conflict between the Greek and Hebrew worldviews. Americans are conflicted. Much of our foundation was hewn from Hebrew (or Biblical) thinking. But to a large extent, modern American culture mirrors the Greek system which extols classic ideals like logic, diversity, wisdom, and observation. Hebrew thought also embraces those values; however, its emphasis is on the concrete rather than the abstract. In Greek thought, contemplation is an end unto itself; whereas the ancient Hebrews saw it as a means by which conclusions could be drawn.

So if you grew up in America, it's no wonder you'd have a hard time getting comfortable with identifying your purpose. In our schools, we emphasize getting a well-rounded education and having a lot of interesting experiences. Now, there's nothing wrong with broadening your horizons. But the distinction that Hebrew thought brings is that all the contemplation leads to specific action items. Life according to the Hebrew mindset is all about the mission described in the Bible.

In contrast, the mantra of modern culture seems to be: prepare for everything to improve your odds of finding something. Rather than stating a clear mission, it encourages us simply to wear clean underwear and keep our fingers crossed. You never know when opportunity may knock.

But it takes audacity to write down a detailed account of what you intend to accomplish in your lifetime. It seems to suggest that you have influence over the future. It may even feel arrogant. Who do we think we are?

When it comes right down to it, most of us don't want to be presumptuous about life. After all, God alone is sovereign. It's much easier just to squelch our ambitions and swallow our daily bread – quietly dreaming, but never boldly reaching. Besides, we're wrong about our lives almost every day. Why humiliate ourselves further by writing it down on paper?

Sure, it sounds like the responsible Christian thing to do. But if we're honest, why bother? Suppose you get hit by a truck next week? So much for your big plans then, eh? Maybe it's more practical just to take life as it comes. After all, that's worked pretty well so far.

Pretty convincing, isn't it? It's no surprise that the people in the pews on Sunday don't understand their calling any better than the unchurched do. They're committed to Christ, but they follow Him with all the intentionality of a wind sock, shifting course whichever

way the breeze blows. Can you imagine if Nehemiah had taken that approach? Or Joshua? Or Paul?

God wants deliberate disciples who understand their purpose, their calling, and their assignment in life. How else are we to stand up to the obstacles we encounter on the way? But if church leaders don't take a stand in their own lives, how can we expect the average Christian to answer the call to intentionality?

So without further delay, let's frame out an approach to help you declare once-and-for-all why you're here.

Purpose

To get the ball rolling, first think in general terms of your broad purpose in the universe. Your purpose is a general statement of the reason(s) God placed you on the earth at this point in time. If you need a hint as to your purpose, take note of God's purposes. What is God up to in the world? Specifically, what is He doing in your generation? In your culture? In your neighborhood? When you start to interpret your life through the lens of what God is accomplishing, things have a way of falling into place.

We are all part of the supporting cast in an epic play. The major theme is God's personal glory and the restoration of man to Himself. What part, then, might a restored one like yourself play in that effort?

The purpose exercise is the least likely to reveal unique and specific functions

There's nothing so influential as the assurance of one's purpose.

You'll never reach your maximum influence until you develop convictions about your purpose in life.

that you will perform in life. It may even sound like a general statement that could apply to almost anyone. But it must not be overlooked. Getting a clear picture of your purpose provides a crucial foundation for the remaining steps.

At first glance, this is such a no-brainer that most people don't bother to think through it. Hence, they ad-lib life instead. But if you spend a few minutes on this one, it's amazing how things can start coming into focus. Once you are able to picture your role in God's plan for the world, your posture changes. The context of your life comes into view. It's easier to maintain perspective and respond wisely when obstacles materialize in your path. You are less likely to place major emphasis on minor issues, clearing the way to focus on what's truly important.

Calling

Next, begin to develop a detailed picture of your special part in God's program. Your calling is a specific statement of a unique role you will fulfill during your lifetime.

We resist stating our calling not because we must declare who we are, but because we must declare who we are not. It forces us to eliminate many other things we'd also like to do in life. Calling defines the net take-away of our little lives. When we declare our calling, we are stating how our mortal lives will be poured out as an offering to God. In the process, we must lay to rest many of our lifelong dreams and ambitions. If God calls you to meet a certain need — and you truly dedicate yourself to that calling — it may mean giving up certain aspects of your lifestyle. There may be professional goals you never fulfill. You may never retire on the beach. Your golf score might never be in the 70s. With sacrifices like that required, it's no wonder our tendency is to put off making a declaration as long as possible.

Understanding your spiritual gifts, special skills, personality, and temperament are essential in identifying your calling. However, don't be intimidated by the science of it. Your intuition goes a long way in assessing your God-given bents.

One of the most often overlooked factors for determining calling is the natural desires of your heart. Many Christians aren't sure what to make of their desires. They understand that the human heart is fundamentally impure. And yet they fail to develop a sense of passion about anything. The fact is that God often places desires in our hearts to compel us toward His plan for our lives. By inviting accountability with other believers and testing our desires against Scripture, we can learn to distinguish between pure desires and impure desires. When we do, this can become a very important guidance system for life.

Of course, desires and giftedness aren't the sole source of evidence of calling. Sometimes our circumstances seem to indicate where God is leading. Neither Moses nor Jonah felt a natural desire toward his calling in life. Their talents didn't make it obvious either. But God used their circumstances to make the path pretty clear.

Once you've attempted to articulate your calling, you should share it with a handful of trusted Christian friends. Invite their candid opinions, and ask for confirmation or redirection.

Assignment

Finally, try to identify the individual tasks that you will perform during your lifetime. An assignment is like a calling, but it pertains to very specific actions or functions you are able to identify; assignments are often the detailed breakdown of a particular calling. Your assignments include the "good works" described in Ephesians 2:10. What has God prepared beforehand so that all you need to do is "walk in it?" As you picture yourself looking back over your life some day, what are some of the highlights that absolutely must take place in order for you to feel like your life was complete? What are the non-negotiable components of your life — without which you could never consider your life a success?

Assignments come in two categories. The first is a fill-or-kill mission, such as a specific task, objective, or accomplishment. For example, your assignment may be to introduce the Gospel to a particular unreached people group. Once the assignment is complete, it's over. You will have fulfilled a unique function in God's kingdom. Like Esther, you will have been created "for such a time as this." Chances are, you will have many such assignments in your lifetime.

The other category describes an ongoing role or function that you perform. This includes things like loving your spouse as Christ loves the church, training your son or daughter in the knowledge of God, or serving the homeless community in your city. These tasks are very specific in nature, yet they may have no clear finish line.

In virtually every case, a person should be able to name numerous assignments for his life. The greatest benefit of taking inventory of your known assignments is that it enables you to prioritize your life's resources accordingly. Everybody has a limited amount of time, energy, money, mental focus, etc. When you have clarity about your purpose and calling, decision-making becomes easy. By eliminating what's not important, you instantly free up vast reserves of your personal resources for what is important. Suddenly, you clear the path to accomplish what really matters.

Maximizing Influence

Without the rudder of purpose and calling in our culture today, goals are like rocket engines without a guidance system. We use goals to propel us from one point to another, but there's no sense of mission in the overall journey. Instead of shooting for strategic goals, we simply exist to max out. The more, the better.

The truth is that you don't have to max out in your life to reach your full potential. In fact, you probably shouldn't. The writer Henry David Thoreau put it this way: "Why should we be in such desperate haste to succeed, and in such desperate enterprises? If a man does not keep pace with his companions, perhaps it is because he hears a different drummer."

Still, there's an even more compelling truth that calls every Christian to invest in this process: discovering your calling is a channel of communication between you and God. The exercise draws us to interact with God as we seek answers His will and direction. This process leads us naturally into the most important conversations of our life.

God not only has the ability to direct your course, but He also has the desire to share that process with you. He wants to relate, heavenly Father to earthly child. Because as you strive to interact with Him in this effort, your relationship will grow. And while He doesn't give us a crystal ball to see the future, He does honor our efforts to plan for it. For this reason, we don't need to be afraid of getting it wrong the first time we try.

Over time, when you know what you're about in life—when your steps are measured with purpose—you will be more efficient and more confident. A sense of influence will follow you. And by delineating the major goals of your earthly existence, you acquire a context for everything you do.

Courage has been defined as "the belief that I am indestructible until my work on earth is done." That's the picture of someone with a clear idea of his purpose and calling. ☐

Adapted from Blueprint for Life, *with permission. (***www.blueprintforlife.com***)*

Ben Ortlip writes books and study curriculum for several prominent Christian authors and oversees creative projects for trend-setting ministries like Campus Crusade for Christ, Injoy, FamilyLife, Walk Thru the Bible, and North Point Ministries. Ben is the co-author of the breakout small group study *Blueprint For Life*. He and his wife, Lisa, live in Cumming, Georgia with their six children.

FOR GROUP DISCUSSION
Use these questions and journal pages to reflect and respond to what you've just read.

1. Based on the approach outlined in this session, how would you articulate your purpose in life?

2. What context does this provide for living out the details of your life?

ERWIN RAPHAEL MCMANUS

CHASING DAYLIGHT

SEIZE THE POWER
OF EVERY MOMENT

Cover image not final

From the Author of UPRISING and THE BARBARIAN WAY

Book Review

TITLE:
Chasing Daylight
AUTHOR:
Erwin Raphael McManus

REVIEW BY:
Michael Auliso

Western culture is filled with carpe diem examples, from seventeenth-century poet Robert Herrick, who encouraged us to "gather ye rosebuds while ye may" to Malcolm Gladwell's bestseller *Blink*, which quantifies how we make important choices in an instant. Erwin Raphael McManus has a few examples too—not to seize a day, or a rosebud … but to grab the brass ring of opportunities. To jump at the chance to honor and reflect God through actions both large and small.

Chasing Daylight (formerly *Seizing Your Divine Moment*) is a hurricane of a book, filled with McManus's passion and sense of urgency as he exhorts us to see that each moment of life holds promise of eternal ramifications. To illustrate the point, McManus reminds us of the Old Testament account of Israel's war with the Philistines recounted in 1 Samuel 13 and 14: vastly outnumbered, Saul's small band of weaponless Hebrews pauses before certain annihilation by the Philistine army. But Saul's son, Jonathan, convinced that God is on Israel's side, acts upon that conviction while his father rests; this feat of faith and courage triggers a rout that ultimately impacts the future of Israel.

Calling this adventurer's inspiration to seize the divine moment "the Jonathan factor," McManus illustrates timeless characteristics that define a life that makes the most of every moment. The notion that living life to the fullest requires risk is not a new one, but *Chasing Daylight* forces us to view the idea with fresh eyes. There is a fine line between living a life of purpose and adventure and living a life of missed opportunity. McManus defines God's will as "a dangerous place to be," and reminds us that there are certain things we do not need a calling to do. "Too many divine opportunities," he writes, "are lost because we keep waiting for a word when the word has already been given."

Chasing Daylight is a great mix of personal experience and anecdotes both humorous and heart-breaking, as well as solid biblical commentary. It's a challenge to step outside the comfort zone and grab each divinely inspired moment. **C**

Blueprint for Life
Creating your own personalized plan to guide you through life

By Ben Ortlip

DISCOVERING GOD'S WILL FOR YOUR LIFE IS DEFINITELY MORE ART THAN SCIENCE. ACTUALLY, IT BEARS CLOSER RESEMBLANCE TO QUANTUM PHYSICS – NOBODY GETS AN A AND ONLY A SELECT FEW SEEM ABLE TO UNDERSTAND IT. AT ANY RATE, GOD DOES HONOR OUR ATTEMPTS TO SEEK HIS WILL FOR OUR LIVES. IN FACT, HE WANTS US TO KNOW. AND WHILE YOU MAY NOT FIND ANY VERSES IN THE BIBLE WITH YOUR NAME IN THEM, THERE ARE SEVERAL CLEAR SIGNALS YOU CAN CONSULT AS YOU SEEK GOD'S PLAN FOR YOUR LIFE.

These beacons offer clues as to what you were created to be and do in life. And they're not hidden in a secret Bible code or cryptic interpretations of ancient prophecy. They're embedded in the fabric of who you are. Just take a look at yourself, and you can learn a lot about your calling in life. God made you. He wired you the way you are on purpose. And He has given you a unique place in the world for a reason.

Creating a blueprint for your life is simply a matter of collecting the right clues and placing them in a central location to use as reference. A blueprint is a rough draft ... a picture of the end product as seen by the Architect. With a blueprint for life, suddenly there is a place to turn for reference when making key decisions. There are written plans to help you recognize when things are on track and when it's time to take the next step in life. There is guidance for establishing a strong foundation, developing your inner wiring, even tending to the cosmetic details. When the house is built according to the plans, it will fulfill every purpose the Architect intended.

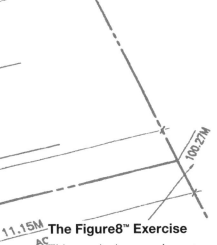

The Figure8™ Exercise

This exercise is one such way to probe for clues about God's intentions when He created you. The exercise explores eight key categories for figuring out God's will for your life. Start by reflecting on these areas that describe your life. You will begin to see common themes that point to God's purpose for your life. Then use the following pages to journal your responses.

PASSION

What makes you passionate? Are there certain things that seem to bring fulfillment or awaken your ambitions? If money were no object, where would you choose to focus your time and energy? These can be important clues as to where God would have you apply yourself.

GIFTEDNESS

What special gifts or skills are you equipped with? Are there abilities that stand out in you which could indicate a function you might perform in the world? What are the things you do best? Is there anything that comes effortlessly for you while others struggle to keep pace? What can you do that no one else can? Sometimes God gives us special talents so that we can perform certain skills that support His master plan.

RESOURCES

What resources or possessions do you have that can be leveraged? Do you have money, a position of influence, a vehicle, or an education that could be a building block for something you pursue? Perhaps you have key relationships with certain people that might be useful in developing one of your passions into an idea, a program, or a business. Could it be that God has given you access to resources that will play an important role in unfolding His plan for your life?

OPPORTUNITIES

What opportunities are sitting on your doorstep today? What opportunities are looming on the horizon? Have new doors opened? Have old ones closed? Might these be an indication of where God is taking you next? Change can be intimidating. But God will often use our circumstances to open doors in our life or to close them.

YOUR PAST

How has God used you in the past? Did it seem like His hand was on your efforts? Which ones were successful? Did you gain valuable experience that would be helpful in a similar arena now? You may already be doing what God wants you to do. And even if you aren't, God almost always gives us a track record that leads logically toward the areas where He will use us in the future. One of the best indicators of the future is often the past.

KEY ENVIRONMENTS

Are there certain environments in which you tend to thrive? Is there a certain area of the country that gets your juices flowing? Do you have a favorite city? Are there particular people or personality types that make you productive? Is there a certain office arrangement or housing situation that enables you to flourish? Sometimes these factors are decided for us, are limited by finances, or must defer to other priorities. But sometimes our preferred environments can lead us toward God's plan for our lives.

GOD'S WORD

There is no place where God has spoken more directly to the issues in our lives than in Scripture. This is the cornerstone of our search for our purpose. Because of God's Word, we don't need to ask if it's God's will for us to cheat on our taxes, or become a drug dealer, or divorce our spouse to marry someone else. In addition to the obvious dos and don'ts, there are many principles that suggest how life is supposed to work. The more you know about Scripture, the easier it is to discern God's will.

WISE COUNSEL

If you were to ask the mentors in your life, what would they say you should do? Preferably, you should ask people you trust, people who have already been where you aspire to go, and people who have nothing to gain or lose by your decision. Iron sharpens iron. If God is leading you toward something, He will often confirm it through the suggestions of others you trust. **C**

The Figure8™ Journal

God uses all of these factors at different times throughout your life. So if you want evidence of what He might have in mind for your future, start by taking a good look at these eight categories. Above all, maintain a prayerful attitude as you work through this exercise. Converse with God, asking Him to show you His will. Ask Him for vision to identify His purpose and calling for your life. Use the spaces following to record your thoughts:

PASSION

GIFTEDNESS

RESOURCES

OPPORTUNITIES

YOUR PAST

KEY ENVIRONMENTS

GOD'S WORD

WISE COUNSEL

Adapted from Blueprint For Life, *by Ben Ortlip. Used by permission.* (**www.blueprintforlife.com**)

BY MARGARET FEINBERG

IDENTITY CRISIS?

AN ETERNAL PERSPECTIVE ON YOUR PERSONAL IDENTITY

AT A CALLING CROSSROADS | ONE OF MY FAVORITE MOMENTS IN THE CLASSIC CHILDREN'S TALE *ALICE IN WONDERLAND* COMES AT THE POINT WHEN ALICE ARRIVES AT A CROSSROADS. SHE NOTICES THE CHESHIRE CAT IN A NEARBY TREE AND ASKS FOR ADVICE AS TO WHICH ROAD SHE SHOULD TAKE.

The cat promptly asks her, "Where do you want to go?"

"I don't know," she admits.

"Then, any road will take you there," the cat responds.

The Cheshire Cat's answer is unexpectedly profound. Knowing where you want to end up has a tremendous impact on the decisions you make along the way. If you don't care where you end up, then all roads are equal. But if you are concerned with God's calling on your life, then here are a few things to keep in mind.

Your primary calling is heavenward. You are called to be like Christ. You are invited to become part of something greater than we can see, touch, or feel. Even people who don't subscribe to Christianity sense this calling or longing or be part of something that is bigger than them. You can see it in the businessman who wants to leave a legacy and the college student who wants to simply make a difference. Something in the very fabric of human nature longs to be part of a story

that lasts beyond us. Yet even with the cry of eternity echoing in our souls, the most important aspect of answering the call is knowing the One who is calling.

Do you know what rests on God's heart for your life day and night? It is not a job or even a career. He desires that you spend eternity with Him. In other words, you are called to be in a life-infusing relationship with Him that will naturally shade your every decision and action.

Your secondary calling manifests itself not only in your relationship with Christ, but also in those you come in contact with and what you do. Followers of Jesus are called to not only know God but to reflect Him to those who don't.

Some people mentioned in Scripture were clearly called for a specific purpose. The Poet-Shepherd-King David was called for the purpose of being king and he fulfilled that calling. His son, Solomon, was called to build the temple. Paul and Barnabas were called to specific missions. Yet many of the people mentioned in the Bible did not have such specific callings. Consider

Jonathan who remained faithful to David as his companion and friend or the role of Aaron in relationship to Moses. Remember the man who opened his home for the disciples to eat their final Passover with Jesus (Mark 14:14-15). Many historians believe this man's home was also used when the disciples waited for the Spirit in the second chapter of Acts. Or take, for example, the friends who were carrying the paralytic to Jesus and unable to get to Him because of the crowd, they removed the roof and lowered him down (Mark 2: 1-4). Even without a note of a specific vocational calling, countless men and women were used by God in mighty and memorable ways.

MISTAKEN IDENTITY

Despite examples from scripture and Jesus' own words, we often find ourselves still confused about our purpose and desperate to discover our calling. What keeps us from walking in the fullness of who God created us to be? It may be a case of mistaken identity.

The film, *The Incredibles*, follows the story of a family of superheroes who have been forced to live normal, anonymous lives after a series of lawsuits against superheroes forced the government to hide them in witness protection programs. Bob Parr, formerly known as Mr. Incredible, lives with his wife Helen, formerly known as Elastigirl, and their children which include invisibility-prone Violet, lightning-quick son Dash, and baby Jack Jack. In their effort to protect their secret identity, Bob works as an insurance claim specialist, Helen acts like the perfect mom, and the three children are told to keep their secret superhero powers to themselves.

But Bob can't resist the temptation to go back to his old life. When he is given the opportunity to be a hero, he jumps at the opportunity but finds himself in a trap set by an old nemesis. In the end, the whole family has to reveal themselves as superheroes in order to save their dad and the planet.

The film is a perfect blend of action adventure and comedy, but underneath the surface, *The Incredibles* touches on deeper issues. At one point in the movie, Elastigirl, a.k.a. Helen, tells her children, "Your identity is your most valuable possession."

Identity is one of the most precious characteristics of being human. Your identity is unique. It not only identifies you, but it helps define who you are. Identity gives us context for life. Knowing your identity is essential: It provides a foundation for how you interact and respond to the world around you.

Yet it's far too easy to allow what you do—whether it's a profession or pastime—to define who you are as a person. You may be a musician, visual artist, scientist, or literary expert. Even if you can tag multiple degrees and awards to your job title, allowing what you do to determine who you are is limiting yourself to a one-dimensional life when you were designed for so much more. You are a living, breathing human being with feelings and emotions and relationships. You have highlights and lowlights, experiencing thrilling moments and the mundane. You eat, sleep, and dream. You smile, laugh and cry. And you are so much more than what takes place behind an office desk or in a cubicle.

Who am I? is one of the biggest questions we'll ever ask ourselves. It challenges our core beliefs—the foundation of who we are as individuals. Unfortunately, our society seems far more concerned with what we do. Think about the last time you attended a gathering with people you

had never met before. After asking for your name and where you're from (if it's not obvious) most people will ask, "What do you do?" From your answer—whether you're working on Wall Street or you're between jobs—people will draw all kinds of conclusions about you. Over time some of these people will get to know you—the real you—but until then your occupation serves as a simple way to label or categorize you in people's minds.

The problem is that it's not just when we meet new people that we allow our professions to define us. Our jobs can easily become the source of our identity. This happens for several reasons. First, defining what you do is much easier than discovering who you really are. It's simpler to stick to shallow labels and generalizations rather than press into the depth and soul-searching required for self-discovery. Second, it takes time to truly know yourself—your likes and dislikes, your passions and fears, your strengths and limitations. There usually isn't time between the transition between school and work for much discovery. You're immediately pigeonholed into a job or career so you end up answering the question What do I do? long before you ever have time to explore the question Who am I? in depth. The result is that your profession overshadows your identity.

The danger in discovering what you want to do with your life before you figure out who you are as an individual is that you can become what you do. Kristie, a 30-year-old veterinarian, has learned this lesson the hard way. She is convinced that what you do from 9 to 5 does not determine who you are as a person. "That is a common mistake," she says. "One that I have made for my whole life. Now

that I am a veterinarian, I realize that I could have worked in so many other ways to help animals and that veterinary medicine is only one possible option. Any other profession might have worked equally well for me and I could have made animals my passion, hobby, or pastime. I would encourage people who can't figure out what they want to be when they grow up that being passionate about your hobbies can be as fulfilling as a good job—maybe even more."

One way to help separate what you do from who you are is to view your vocation and passion in broader terms. Instead of defining yourself as a third grade elementary teacher, recognize that your gift and talent is teaching and that's something that can be used in countless professions. That way when you change jobs or enter a new stage of life, you are open to the different ways God can use you in a new environment. When you embrace a broad definition of what you do, then the possibilities of using your talents and gifts is expanded exponentially.

The security of knowing our identity in Christ frees us up to live out our calling to be on mission with God's agenda. **C**

Adapted from What The Heck Am I Going To Do With My Life*, Copyright © 2005 by Margaret Feinberg, Tyndale House Publishers. Used by permission.*

Margaret Feinberg is author more than a dozen books including *What the Heck am I Going to Do With My Life: Pursue Your Passion, Find the Answer, Twentysomething: Surviving & Thriving in the Real World*, and *God Whispers: Learning to Hear His Voice*. She lives in Juneau, Alaska, with her 6'8" Norwegian husband Leif.

THE MOST IMPORTANT ASPECT OF ANSWERING THE CALL IS KNOWING THE ONE WHO IS CALLING.

Journal

What does COURAGEOUS IN CALLING mean to me?

THINK

ENGAGED in Culture

How do I respond to the cultural context we are living in?

As a leader, I must understand the context God has placed me in. I must know the audience I am connecting with to have any opportunity of relevance. Because God desires that Christ-followers engage and influence their surroundings, I will be a source of hope, redemption, justice and peace in my community, demonstrating a piece of the Kingdom of God in a fallen world.

At the Borders of Culture
Discovering ministry vision at your corner bookstore

By Rick James

Next Generation Leader is to translate biblical truth to a culture, but... Failure to identify it is the difference between a "voice... ...and a "voice speaking to the wilderness:" a ministry o... ...rendered innocuous and trivial.

THE ROLE OF A NEXT GENERATION LEADER IS TO TRANSLATE BIBLICAL TRUTH TO A CULTURE, BUT CULTURE IS A CHAMELEON. FAILURE TO IDENTIFY IT IS THE DIFFERENCE BETWEEN A "VOICE CALLING FROM THE WILDERNESS," AND A "VOICE SPEAKING TO THE WILDERNESS;" IT'S THE DIFFERENCE BETWEEN A MINISTRY OF LEVERAGE AND IMPACT VERSUS A VOICE RENDERED INNOCUOUS AND TRIVIAL.

Over the years, I've spoken or done ministry on as many as 150 campuses. In the world of youth ministry, that's not so much a byline as it is an epitaph. If I have learned one thing ministering at "the fountain of youth" it is that relevance is maintained by swimming in the ever-flowing stream of cultural ideas.

The whole idea of "in the world, not of it" often causes leaders in ministry to shy away from engaging in cultural trends and view. The fact is, while the vision and mission of the Church—and the message

and hope of Christ—are timeless, our methods for communicating them must be relevant with the times.

CULTURAL CUES FROM THE APOSTLE PAUL

"For as I walked around and looked carefully at your objects of worship, I even found an altar with this inscription: TO AN UNKNOWN GOD." (Acts 17:23 NIV)

The apostle Paul was master of cultural relevance. From this account, we can imagine him in Athens, spending an af-

ternoon window-shopping ... observing the culture, gathering ideas, and then sorting them out. All this to be able to speak directly to the Athenian people: refuting their errant views, borrowing from their own culture, and commandeering all manner of Athenian bricolage to build an on-ramp to the gospel.

What if Paul were here today? How would he employ this strategy of engagement? My guess is he'd spend the afternoon at Borders. Because let's face it, a great place to find culturally relevant ideas is at your corner bookstore. If you learn to observe, gather, and sort ideas at Borders, you'll always be on the crest of the cultural wave. So, let me guide you through an afternoon trip to Borders. Just like Paul, we'll be able to recycle much of what we learn. Our strategy is to first observe and gather information, and then we'll sort it out through a shelving method in order to apply it to our leadership and ministry.

THE BUSINESS SECTION

I've seen Jack Welch's face 18 times, so we must have arrived in the business section. Look, here's Malcolm Gladwell's new book *Blink*. *A tennis coach always knows when a player will double fault. … An art historian spots a fraud not discernable to computers.* … We find a dozen other case studies to back Gladwell's thesis that the intuitive wisdom of trained and experienced professionals is more valuable than mountains of research or the pooled ignorance of a focus group or committee. Branded the new corporate guru, Gladwell's ideas are shaping corporate America.

Is this useful research to have at the ready? I don't know … ever felt through your years of experience that you possibly knew better than the church committee or council which way was forward, and that it would be best to just trust your gut? Well then, I guess that answers that. There's more here, but we're a little

underdressed for the business section so let's join the retired and out-of-work over in History.

THE HISTORY SECTION

Oh look, another page-turner on Ulysses S. Grant, and it's the size of the Manhattan phonebook. That's not what we're looking for. We're shopping for new ideas. Here's how we find them: First, is there anyone we should be aware of? A new biography about someone who might have, or will be, gaining cultural influence? (I think Grant's stranglehold on public opinion is clearly on the decline.)

You ask, "Couldn't we find this out by watching the news?" Yes, but books are more reliable. Publishers like making money—lots of it—and they don't invest in a book unless they think there's an audience. So note who's become worthy of a publisher's investment, as it's likely to be a trend. I'm not seeing any new authors, but in terms of new ideas, *The Punch* demonstrates the new way to tell history through the micro-event. It's the idea that everything leading up to, surrounding, and resulting from, a specific action or event. For example, the French and Indian War can be traced back to a singular insult.

Let's stick this idea in the shopping cart because it could be commandeered in preaching from the Old Testament—the

story of David and Bathsheba could be traced back to … *The Glance*.

Hold on … I just hit paydirt. *Five Quarts: A Personal and Natural History of Blood*. As the Old Testament is drenched in the crimson fluid, the thoughts contained here may provide genuine insight as well as preaching fodder. I might actually buy this one or the book next to it, *The History of the World in Six Glasses*. Finding an organizing principle on which to divide history is a crazy-maker, and this author, bless his barstool, has lined it up by drinks. Now why is this an idea worth noticing? Well, we currently live in a culture of speed: fast-paced information for a fast-paced life. We feed the culture of speed at the coffee shops found on every corner. A double espresso the drug of choice. The ideas in this book might make a beautiful introduction to a biblical series on our culture of speed.

As you move deeper into the rows and rows of ideas, you get faster at stripping useful kernels. But we've spent too long here so we need to either buy the memoir of Ulysses S. Grant or get back to browsing. Let's move over to fiction.

THE FICTION SECTION

Fiction for me is like bran, which I only consume because it's good for my colon. In the two-story barn of Borders you'll

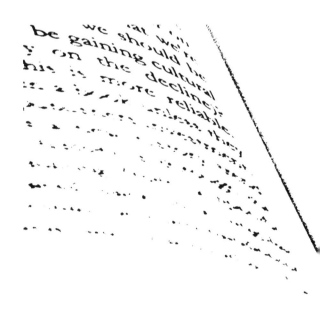

find both high culture and popular culture works of fiction. Pop culture provides immediate, quick, and flashy ideas. High culture, on the other hand, is slower and requires that you enter in … and in many cases tolls your patience. The taste for high culture is an acquired one, which describes why I loathe it. High culture does have gravitas, as it is weighty in topics and ideas. Leaders must always peck away at great writing and literature, because those who dabble only in pop culture will simply congregate and cultivate shallow followers.

Everyone should read the obvious classics; however, you will be left in awe by the talents of some of these more contemporary fiction writers: Philip Roth, Don DeLillo, Flannery O'Conner (Christian), John Updike, Alice Munro, Rick Moody, Annie Dillard (Christian), Ian McEwan, Annie Proulx, or Tobias Wolf. Moving on …

THE NPR SECTION
One of the treasure troves in the bookstore is the section entitled "In the Media" or "On NPR."

In this section, media programmers have done the legwork of idea filtering. They've looked at the landscape of ideas and identified these as looming largest on the cultural horizon. Take careful inventory of what you find here. With most

books, the jacket cover and table of contents provide a sufficient map of where the ride is heading.

THE RELIGION/ SPIRITUALITY SECTION
We've now moved into the Religion/ Spirituality section. I don't come to Borders to harvest Christian thought any more than Paul was learning Christian theology in downtown Athens. Rather, I come here to get the pulse of spirituality in our culture. The fad for today's celebrities is promoting their religion of choice, like Kabbalah and Scientology. You'll no doubt find the popularity of spiritual exploration reflected in the diversity of religious literature.

Hmm, now here's something interesting: M. Scott Peck (not a bastion of orthodoxy) has a new book, *Glimpses of the Devil*, apparently delving into issues of possession and exorcism. I'm not sure of specifics yet, but the idea of a Halloween outreach on campus and material from this book are two sticks I immediately begin to rub together in my mind. When the smoke clears, I may have myself an evangelistic talk … or just a lot of smoke.

THE SCIENCE SECTION
Let's take a quick peek in the science section. Of course, we do so knowing of the ongoing battle between those who see God's hand in the universe and those

who don't. The debate has raged for eons; however new findings from DNA, microbiology, and astronomy have provided tremendous ammunition for Christians on the question of God's existence. Generally speaking, every year authors like Dawkins and Gould write books with titles like *Blind Watchmaker* or *You're Simply a Hairball Coughed Up by a Random Universe*, and writers like Behe, Dembski, and Denton point the way toward an intelligent designer. At the popular level, Lee Strobel's *Case for a Creator* is a great overview of the issue. Christians have made tremendous headway in this battle, so unless a new book causes a ripple in the universe debate, I'll just button up my lab coat, put my pen back in its pocket protector, and keep moving.

THE NEW NON-FICTION SECTION
The most valuable books by far do not have their own category, but pop up in the new non-fiction section before they are dispatched to their appropriate phylum and genus. Many belong under social sciences/sociology. They are written by authors who are able to connect the dots of cultural indicators, cross-pollinate knowledge from various disciplines, and bring forth predictive analysis. The antiquated term for such meta-thinkers was "renaissance man" (or woman). Today they sometimes go by the label "futurists."

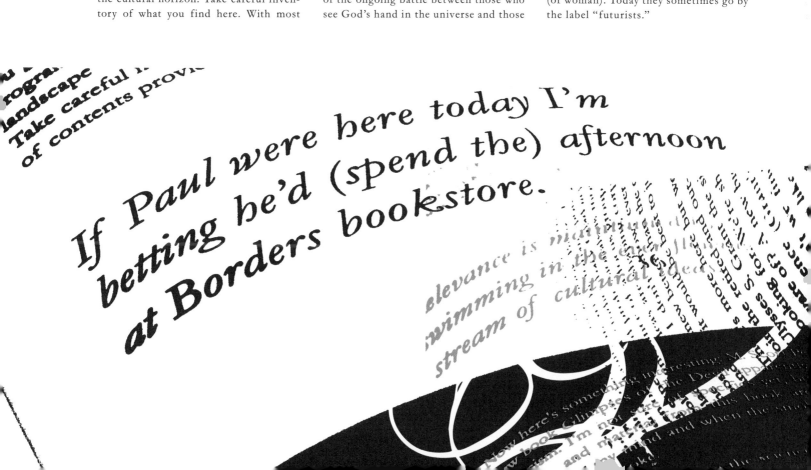

If Paul were here today I'm betting he'd (spend the) afternoon at Borders bookstore.

session

truth to a cul...
...rence between a...
"wilderness," a mir...
...vial.

...y an ISO campuses...
...it to an epitaph, f...
...never far awa...

High culture has gravitas, it is weighty and leaders who dabble only in pop will simply congregate and cultivate shallow followers, which is why you will be left in awe at great writing and literature. The classics to read should be the... you will be left in awe by the talents of some of these more conte... ...dance: Philip Roth, Don DeLillo, Flannery O'Conner (Christian), ... Alice Munro, Rick Moody, Annie Dillard (Christian), Ian McEwan, ... or Tobias Wolf.

One of the anxious moves in the bookstore is the section entitled ...
..."On NPR." (NPR's Fresh Air, is one of the great sieves of influ...
...in the NPR website you can download the broadcasts.) In this...

I'm looking at three new books by well-known "big thinkers." *The World is Flat* is Thomas Friedman's third book on globalization. No one understands and explains the emerging interdependent world and its implications better than Friedman, so if Friedman writes it, I read it (or at least say that I did). The two others are *Collapse: How Societies Choose to Fail or Succeed* by Pulitzer winner Jared Diamond, and *Freakonomics: A Rogue Economist Explores the Hidden Side of Everything* by Levitt and Dubner. For all I know these books could be horrendous … but do you see the type of book I'm trying to describe? They provide a compass to the culture by synthesizing enormous amounts of data and trends. These books are conceptual gold.

DON'T FORGET THE MAGAZINE RACK

Well, our shopping cart is about full with ideas, but before leaving we should scan the magazine rack. Opinions vary on what magazines best keep you on the cultural cusp. Personally, I always look at *Wired*, *Fast Company*, *Time*, *Newsweek*, *Entertainment*, and *Oxygen/Wallpaper* (the latest in design, art, and architecture). But this brings us back to the question, "Why is Borders the best stethoscope to hear the heartbeat of culture? Why books and magazines over the internet, movies, or television?"

Clearly all the mentioned venues provide cultural insights—some indispensable—but books and magazines consolidate an enormous amount of divergent ideas all in one location. The internet is a billion cultural niches with few "Central Stations" for ideas. The exception, of course, are blogs or webzines (*The Wall Street Opinion Journal*, *Plastic*, or *Slate* for example), but most of these are confined to a single subject such as politics or entertainment. Also, remember we said that in order to get into print, an idea has had to demonstrate it is more than a social hiccup. Otherwise publishers wouldn't invest the ink and paper. Content is king.

Movies and television do possess something that can't be garnered from a book: emotional memory. For example, when I mention to you Frodo's struggle in *The Lord Of the Rings*, I tap into the emotions that the film producers so excessively cultivated through music, sound, and story. While books and magazines provide me with a palette of ideas that I can use to influence, movies and television offer opportunities for emotional connection.

OUT THE DOORS AND INTO CULTURE

I leave Borders with several shopping bags full of ideas (I use plastic instead of paper, for everything I've taken is recyclable). As we take these books and ideas home, we'll need to file them on the proper shelf for easy reference. What I mean is that we'll create a context in which to use these engaging ideas.

CONTAMINANTS SHELF

The first cabinet is for poisons and cultural toxins. As Paul was aware of, and addressed, the Athenians distorted thought patterns, and we should do the same. Borders is in fact filled with a billion venomous ideas, any of which could be spiritually lethal in the wrong dose. I would put Dan Brown's *The Da Vinci Code* on this shelf. As a shepherd, I'm on the look-out for dangerous ideas that are having, or could have, a significant influence on the culture and therefore on those to whom I minister. I am not a prophet. I don't know what trends or ideas will ever become a Class-5 cultural storm, but if I know what's off the coast, sitting in warm waters and picking up speed, I can take the steps to prepare for or prevent damage.

CORPORATE SHELF

Gladwell's *Blink!* goes on the second shelf for corporate ideas. I always sample the fruit of the business session, because while the Church is definitely a family and a mission, its administrative and leadership structure functions much like a corporation. There are ideas in business that help me lead and influence amidst the corporate functions of ministry. This is why I think every leader should read *Good to Great* by Jim Collins.

CONVERSATION SHELF

While Paul was cramming specifically for an upcoming evangelistic exam at the Areopagus, my reasons for gathering are a little broader. I shelve some ideas for no other reason than that it aids in social proficiency. Ministry is relationships, relationships are built through conversation, and ideas fuel conversation. Lousy conversation is usually symptomatic of a lack of knowledge or narrow minds and the prescription is a book jacket.

COMMANDEER SHELF

"'For in him we live and move and have our being.' As some of your own poets have said, 'We are his offspring.'" (Acts 17:28 NIV)

Ideas have the power to influence. They sit hostage on the shelves of Borders awaiting liberation. There are a million ideas flying aimlessly around Borders. I look to hijack and commandeer them for use in ministry as Paul did in Athens. I'll be glad to put to kingdom service the five years someone spent researching *The History of Blood*, whatever their motive for doing so. Capturing history through the lens of a micro-moment like *The Punch* … that's brilliant! Hand it over, along with your other valuables, and I'll put it on my shelf for future use … and I'll be sure to include you in the footnotes.

CONVERSION SHELF

The apostle Paul scoured the city for raw material (ideas) that could be processed into a culturally relevant presentation of the gospel. Borders is filled with such bridges to the culture.

I'm sure there are other shelf categories, but none that begin with the letter "C" so we'll keep it to five. Here's a closing question to ponder: Would Paul's speech to the Areopagus have been blessed even if he hadn't done his homework on Athenian culture? I'll let you wrestle with that, but I will note that we will never know for sure, because Paul did, in fact, do his homework.

Over the next few weeks, spend an afternoon gathering ideas at Borders or Barnes & Noble, or your local corner bookstore. Using these five general categories, begin to brainstorm ways you can use cultural trends as a tool for engaging others in the truth of Jesus Christ. **C**

Rick James has served with Campus Crusade for Christ nearly twenty years and is currently a conference speaker and the Publisher of *CruPress*. His MDiv. is from Trinity Evangelical Divinity school and is the author of two books: *Flesh* and *Postcards from Corinth*.

FOR GROUP DISCUSSION
USE THESE QUESTIONS AND JOURNAL PAGES TO REFLECT AND
RESPOND TO WHAT YOU'VE JUST READ.

1. On a scale of 1-10, how important is it to keep up with cultural trends?

2. Of the recent cultural ideas and trends you are aware of, which do you feel to be the most spiritually dangerous?

3. What was a recent event within culture that you attempted to relate to the gospel? How did you relate it?

4. *Where or how do you currently keep up with what's happening within the culture?*

5. *Name two influential non-Christian books you've read or skimmed, and explain how they influenced you.*

DEEP DIVE
Download a complete smallgroup leader's guide at **www.catalystgroupzine.com**

For more on our role in culture, see Mattthew 5:13-16 and 1 Peter 2:16. Check out Jesus' commission to engage culture in Matthew 28:18-20. Jesus also offers His greatest commandment as a strategy for engaging others in Matthew 22:36-39 and 1 John 3:16-18.

CANDID with
Brian McLaren

CATALYST: You wrote a book called *A New Kind of Christian*. Give us some insight into what this book is about.

MCLAREN: I believe we are living in a very exciting and challenging time—a very important time in the plotline of Christianity. It is similar to a time five hundred years ago when Christianity existed in a relatively stable form called "Medieval Christianity." It existed in this form for close to one thousand years.

Five hundred years ago, though, the scientific worldview of the Middle Ages started to fall apart. The economic and political structures were under threat as new intellectual currents developed. Christians began to wonder if their faith would be able to detach from the medieval culture to which it was so closely linked. Could Christianity survive the fall of the Middle Ages and re-engage to help create a new world? Some think it did. We call that new world, in which we live today, the modern world.

I believe we are at a similar time as then. This modern world is similarly fraying as the medieval world did. The coherence that holds the modern world together is becoming incoherent and fragmented.

A New Kind of Christian suggests we have a new challenge. We are living in two worlds—one that is fading and another that is emerging—and that is not easy. The question is, can the Christian faith disengage, once again, from this world and take on the next challenge?

CATALYST: The introduction of the book recounts a story about you listening to Christian radio in your car. You were frustrated with the things you were hearing. Can you expound on that?

MCLAREN: This was about ten years ago during what I consider the hardest time in my life. It was a three year period of spiritual crisis you might call a dark night of the soul. I was grappling with Christianity's disengagement, and in the midst of these struggles, I remember driving down the road with a Christian radio station on. A preacher came on and spoke at length about a number of things with absolute certainty. Then, the next preacher came on saying just the opposite with equal certainty, and then the next came on and did the same. I complained to my wife about this and she said that I'd bet-

ter stop listening to Christian radio—it was making me a much worse Christian.

I'm not blaming the preachers on the radio, but I was struggling with this concept. Something happens when you spend a great deal of time in community, Christian or otherwise. You start to see more. It is like the early stages of dating when you think the person you're with is practically perfect in every way. Then, you meet their family and you discover their family is weird. Later it occurs to you that the person you are dating is making the same conclusions about your family. The rose-colored glasses are off. The same happens in Christian community; you face the weirdness of your Christian family.

Our challenge is how we deal with this. We have to sort through it all and be honest about the junk and the barnacles so that we can scrape the grime off the surface and look for what really matters. We are not Christians because of other Christians. We are Christians because of Christ. We must always be able maintain the core of our faith which is Jesus.

CATALYST: In *A New Kind of Christian*, you chose to write in story form. Why did you choose that?

MCLAREN: When my first book came out, I received the best reviews I will ever likely receive. The one that stood out, though, was a negative review of the book that I found very perceptive. The critic wrote, "If McClaren means what he's saying, he shouldn't be writing non-fiction, he should be writing fiction." I remember thinking that there was truth to that, but I didn't feel ready to write fiction yet.

When I started writing *A New Kind of Christian*, it was non-fiction. I was 160 pages into it and five percent though my outline when I realized I would have a 600 page book if I continued the way I was going. I decided to try to tell it as a story.

I learned a number of things though the process of writing fiction, but one I found particularly important. We all need to think. We need to think deeply. We all want easy answers and formulas. We're resistant to deep thought. I realized by working with a fictional story that the characters could be in conversation. They didn't always agree. They pushed back at each other. By having these conversations

in the book, I felt I would stimulate more thinking than by simply trying to make my point.

CATALYST: The book is called *A New Kind of Christian*, but isn't the new kind of Christian just getting back to the old kind of Christian in some ways?

MCLAREN: I've heard this argument before. People will tell me that we don't need a new kind of Christian, we need an old kind of Christian. I agree in a certain sense. Only, it is not that simple. Some refer to the 1950s when they say old. Others mean the 1750s, AD 34, or some golden age of the past. Has Christianity ever reached an ideal time for everyone?

I understand that we do not want to lose our connection to our heritage. That is especially important if we are approaching another major shift in culture. Many of the resources we will need and the lessons we will learn from will require us to look back to the Middle Ages and the early centuries of the church. We need to learn from and delve into the past, but we must continue to travel forward. We're at a place in the road where we face new obstacles and barriers. It's important to know where we've been, but these new challenges require some mid-course corrections for all of us.

CATALYST: Many church leaders care greatly about seeing the church regain ground in today's world. What would you say to them?

MCLAREN: First, be careful. The movie *Spiderman* said it best: "With much power comes much responsibility." He was echoing Jesus' words, "Those to whom much is given, from them much is expected." As Christians with some role in America, we must be careful of how we steward so much power. History tells us that there was a time when those who disagreed with a sermon could have been put in jail or tormented by religious authority. Terrible things were done in the name of religion. We must be careful, especially as Christians who live in the most powerful nation in the world.

But there are things of far more value to regain than power or authority – credibility, authenticity, and integrity. I was watching religious television last night and I couldn't help but think, "I hope none of my friends are watching this,"

"CHRISTIAN LEADERS MUST HELP REGAIN THE LOST INTEGRITY, HUMILITY AND CHRIST-LIKENESS THAT IS SO DESPERATELY NEEDED IN CHRISTIANITY TODAY."

because there was a lost credibility and authenticity there. Christian leaders must help regain the lost integrity, humility, and Christ-likeness that is so desperately needed in Christianity today. We must actually believe that God is with us in every affair of our daily lives. We're charged to live authentically, be a good neighbor and go out of our way to interact with people who are nothing like us socially, ethnically, or religiously. This is what Jesus did and there are no shortcuts to it.

CATALYST: How do we evangelize in this context?

MCLAREN: Very often we count conversions and ask questions like, "How many people have you led to Christ," and "How many people have been saved in your ministry?" Counting can fit into certain framework, but counting is also dangerous because it results in seeing people as commodities. When we dehumanize people like this, we turn them into notches on a belt rather than people for whom Christ died. If we treat the most important and best news in the world as a sales pitch, people will see it as inauthentic and cheap. If we can connect with people as friends and bring them into our lives where they can see the love of Christ in us, they will be drawn to Christ, not just our over-rehearsed spiel.

But first, in order to meet these people, Christians have to get out more. We are so wrapped up in our comfortable church world that we do not have any friends who are not in the faith. What would happen if we did the church thing a little less and lived the Gospel a little more? Those that need Christ the most are not sitting next to you on Sunday.

CATALYST: What would you say to a leader who is today where you were ten years ago? They are going through the motions every day but are stuck in a mold they are struggling to get out of.

MCLAREN: These are not easy times to be a spiritual leader of any type. We are torn by the expectations of those who want to preserve the 1950s or the 1970s, but often our desire is to create churches that can actually mean something to our peers, friends, and neighbors. Let's recognize that it is not easy and never has been. Here are two things we have to do.

1. We must learn to be a friend to ourselves. Abraham Lincoln was quoted to say that after he had disposed of the duties of his office, he hoped that, even if he lost every other friend in the world, he would have conducted himself in such a way that he was still a friend to himself. Many of us are kinder to everyone else than we are to ourselves. We accept other's expectations of us and push ourselves to meet them. We have to learn how to treat ourselves with some gentleness and kindness. Sometimes that means we have to take a vacation, a day off, or just a long walk alone.

2. We have to find people who we can "know" with. We think of knowing as something that happens inside of our own brain, but knowing is more of a social act. In Ephesians chapter three, Paul says, "I pray that you may know the height and depth and breadth of the love of God, that you may know this with all the saints." (verses 17-18) We all need, as John Eldredge would say, a band of brothers, a few close friends who we can be honest with, think with, growth with, and know with.

CATALYST: What is one thing you want to say to next generation leaders?

MCLAREN: After walking with Christ for more than thirty years through mistakes and troubles, I believe this more than I ever have: God is truly good and you can trust that he is with you whatever you're going through. You have never had a thought about God that is better than God actually is. God is wonderful, and everything you can do to open your soul to the goodness and love of our God will humble your heart and help you become the person God wants you to be. Remember that and walk with God. **C**

Brian McLaren is founder of Cedar Ridge Community Church, an innovative church near Washington, D.C. He is the author of *A New Kind of Christian*, *Finding Faith*, *The Story We Find Ourselves In*, and *A Generous Orthodoxy*. Brian is affiliated with Emergent, a growing generative friendship among missionary Christian leaders. He and his wife, Grace, have four children. For more information, visit **www.anewkindofchristian.com**.

TRUE STORY

XXX CHURCH

In the Gutter

What are two pastors doing with a pornographer? That was the question coming from all angles when Mike Foster and Craig Gross teamed up with James DiGiorgio, a famous pornography producer, to shoot a 30-second anti-porn commercial.

The commercial, part of Foster and Craig's **XXXChurch.com** campaign against pornography, gained nation-wide media attention, not to mention scrutiny from Christians who didn't appreciate Foster and Craig's associations. The young pastors, however do not waver from their efforts. "The reality is this is exactly what Jesus would be dealing with today. He was a controversial figure and we're okay with being controversial figures," said Foster.

Working with Jimmy D. is an example of exactly what these two California pastors and their ministry stand for. Months after first meeting DiGiorgio, they received an email from him offering to produce, film and edit XXXchurch.com's next commercial at absolutely no charge. They never hesitated. "I don't think my faith is meant only for me—it's something I'm supposed to share and show to the rest of the world, including veteran pornographers like James DiGiorgio, who sees what I have and realizes how integral it is to my life," said Gross.

Foster and Gross are passionate about living in the trenches of this spiritual battle. In addition to their savvy website and controversial commercials, Foster and Gross take their message to pornography conventions, which is where they first met Jimmy D. "Frankly, all the hoopla about our relationship [with Jimmy D.] is a sad commentary on the Church's performance when it comes to getting in the gutter. This type of thing is exactly what Christians should be doing, and the only reason we made so much news is because most Christians aren't doing it."

XXXChurch.com promotes itself as the number one Christian porn website—a clever way to grab the attention of anyone surfing the Web or looking for a couple of pastors unafraid to engage a culture that isn't so squeaky clean. To download a few accountability tool for the internet, visit **www.x3watch.com** today. **C**

TRUE STORY

Creating Culture

ANDREA ROSSELLE

Andrea Rosselle is a juggler of sorts. Not the circus juggler you may be picturing, but a juggler of the Church and the art world. Employed by the Houston church called Ecclesia, Andrea is both an artist and a believer—a believer who is "invigorated by a hope and desire to see the arts find a home within the Christian community and artists challenged to create unabashedly in their beautiful gifting from God." (**www.ecclesiahouston.org**)

Andrea feels completely at home at Ecclesia, where the first value stated on its website reads: "Beauty, art, and creativity are valued, utilized and understood as coming from our Creator." Andrea feels a kinship with the community there, adding, "These are my people . . . a people who are beautifully broken with the tendency to flounder and sprint towards a God they can't always define."

Through her involvement with the Xnihilo Art Gallery established by the church, Andrea sees Ecclesia more and more engaged with its community. "Engaging culture is engaging men and women at the height of their decadence and the depth of their poverty—and loving them with open arms." She says, "It is less about why we all watch Harry Potter, Star Wars, and Lord of the Rings, and more about who you are watching it with."

Her local church seems to be engaging culture through the arts, but what about Christianity as a whole? Andrea believes it is rapidly growing, "but yet is still inching slowly in the sights of history," she says. "We as a larger community need to embrace not just the visual image, but those laboring to create it. I implore others to have the conversations that move individuals toward embracing what they may not understand. Supporting artists on a spiritual, emotional, and financial level will bring forth the passionate pursuit of those artists towards the glory of God."

Sure, there's tension in that, but Andrea embraces the example of Jesus. After all, "Jesus is there in that tension," she says, "not to condemn but to love."

A new idea? Not really. Andrea reminds us, "Impacting culture is as age-old as loving your neighbor." **C**

Photo by Todd Graves

TRUE STORY

GIFT CARD GIVER.COM

Creating New Ways to Give to Others

Heather Locy and Andre Shinabarger have discovered a way to "pick pockets" and reclaim billions of dollars of wasted money.

Their theory is simple: A growing number of people are carrying around unused money left on gift cards in their wallets. Typically, the amounts are so small that consumers overlook them and end up never redeeming them. The idea of Locy and Shinabarger is to collect these gift cards—of any value—and donate them in large quantities to organizations that can use them to help those in need.

Their organization is called **GiftCardGiver.com**. And it all started with a small group of friends with a common passion for giving and helping others.

Heather says, "As Christians we often only give to our local church and as a result we miss out on helping some really good organizations. GiftCardGiver is a great way to increase our giving outside of our churches without taking money away from the local church."

Because they're keeping it simple, Heather and Andre are able to watch GiftCardGiver make an impact without having to put their lives on hold in the meantime.

Heather, a busy wife and mother of two young boys, intentionally cultivates friendships with nonbelievers, avoiding the Christian "bubble" or "cocoon" that easily separates many of us from the real world. She credits GiftCardGiver as the catalyst for some great conversations between Christians and non-Christians revolving around social injustices. "Rather than separating ourselves somehow," she says, "a more effective way to impact the world in which we live is to just be 'in the world, but not of it.' We're perceived as more credible that way."

Andre is a married student training to be a Physician's Assistant. Like Heather, she surrounds herself with non-Christian friends, engaging them in meaningful conversations about life and meaning. "I love to challenge current thinking 'religiosity' and what it means to be a new kind of Christian," she says. "I think it's critical to not stay trapped in the 'Christian ghetto,' but to open your mind and heart to all people and worldviews."

Both Heather and Andre hope that through GiftCardGiver.com, and the involvement with common good organizations, all people will be drawn to the compassion of Christ for those in need. **G**

YOUR STORY

Engaging the culture is the mandate for redeeming our generation. Think of leaders, both historically and today, who are examples in engaging our culture for Christ. What were/are their strategies? How are you engaging and having conversations in your own community? What stories will people tell of how you transformed culture?

TOTAL TRUTH

Liberating Christianity from Its Cultural Captivity

By Nancy Pearcey

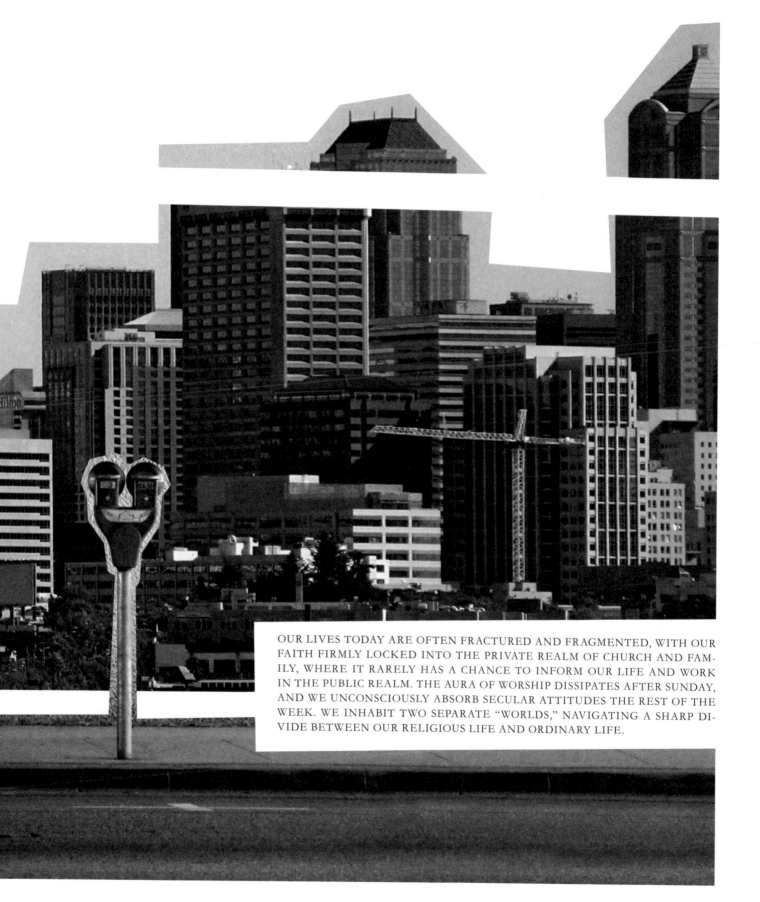

OUR LIVES TODAY ARE OFTEN FRACTURED AND FRAGMENTED, WITH OUR FAITH FIRMLY LOCKED INTO THE PRIVATE REALM OF CHURCH AND FAMILY, WHERE IT RARELY HAS A CHANCE TO INFORM OUR LIFE AND WORK IN THE PUBLIC REALM. THE AURA OF WORSHIP DISSIPATES AFTER SUNDAY, AND WE UNCONSCIOUSLY ABSORB SECULAR ATTITUDES THE REST OF THE WEEK. WE INHABIT TWO SEPARATE "WORLDS," NAVIGATING A SHARP DIVIDE BETWEEN OUR RELIGIOUS LIFE AND ORDINARY LIFE.

Most believers find this highly frustrating. We really want to integrate our faith into every aspect of life, including our profession. We want to be whole people—people of integrity.

ABSOLUTELY DIVINE:
The "Ultimate Principle"

If you press any set of ideas back far enough, eventually you reach some starting point. Every system of thought begins with some ultimate principle. If it does not begin with God, it will begin with some dimension of creation—the material, the spiritual, the biological, the empirical, or whatever. Some aspect of created reality will be put forth as the ground and source of everything else.

To use religious language, this ultimate principle functions as the divine, if we define that term to mean the one thing upon which all else depends for existence. This starting assumption has to be accepted by faith, not by prior reasoning. (Otherwise it is not really the ultimate starting point for all reasoning—something else is, and we have to dig deeper and start there instead.)

Even nonbelievers hold to some ultimate ground of existence, which functions as an idol or false god. Faith is a universal human function, and if it is not directed toward God it will be directed toward something else.

It is not as though Christians have faith, while secularists base their convictions purely on facts and reason. Secularism itself is based on ultimate beliefs, just as much as Christianity is. Some part of creation—usually matter or nature—functions in the role of the divine. So the question is not which view is religious and which is purely rational; the question is which is true and which is false.

Ever since the Fall, the human race has been divided into two distinct groups—those who follow God and submit their minds to His truth and those who set up an idol of some kind and then organize their thinking to rationalize their worship of that idol. Over time, as people's ultimate commitments shape the choices they make, their perspective is inevitably molded to support those choices. A false god leads to the formation of a false worldview. This is why Christians cannot complacently abandon so-called secular

subject areas to nonbelievers. Instead we must identify and critique the dominant intellectual idols and then construct biblically based alternatives.

A set of ideas for interpreting the world is like a philosophical toolbox, stuffed with terms and concepts. If Christians do not develop their own tools of analysis, then when some issue comes up that they want to understand, they'll reach over and borrow someone else's tools—whatever concepts are generally accepted in their professional field or in the culture at large. Not only do we fail to be salt and light to a lost culture, but we ourselves may end up being shaped by that culture.

BIBLICAL TOOLBOX:
The Big-Picture Perspective

How do we make sure our toolbox contains biblically based conceptual tools for every issue we encounter? We must begin by being utterly convinced that there is a biblical perspective on everything—not just on spiritual matters. The Old Testament tells us repeatedly that "The fear of the LORD is the beginning of wisdom" (Ps. 111:10; Prov. 1:7; 9:10; 15:33). Similarly, the New Testament teaches that in Christ are "all the treasures of wisdom and knowledge" (Col. 2:3). We often interpret these verses to mean spiritual wisdom only, but the text places no limitation on the term. "Most people have a tendency to read these passages as though they say that the fear of the Lord is the foundation of religious knowledge," writes philosopher Roy Clouser. "But the fact is that they make a very radical claim—the claim that somehow all knowledge depends upon religious truth."[1]

All belief systems work the same way. As we saw earlier, whatever a system puts forth as self-existing is essentially what it regards as divine. And that religious commitment functions as the controlling principle for everything that follows. The fear of some "god" is the beginning of every proposed system of knowledge.

Once we understand how first principles work, then it becomes clear that all truth must begin with God. The only self-existent reality is God, and everything else depends on Him for its origin and continued existence. Nothing exists apart from His will; nothing falls outside the scope of the central turning points in biblical history: Creation, Fall, and Redemption.

Creation

The Christian message does not begin with "accept Christ as your Savior;" it begins with "in the beginning God created the heavens and the earth." The Bible teaches that God is the sole source of the entire created order. No other gods compete with Him; no natural forces exist on their own; nothing receives its nature or existence from another source. Thus His word, or laws, or creation ordinances give the world its order and structure. God's creative word is the source of the laws of physical nature, which we study in the natural sciences. It is also the source of the laws of human nature—the principles of morality (ethics), of justice (politics), of creative enterprise (economics), of aesthetics (the arts), and even of clear thinking (logic). That's why Psalm 119:91 says, "all things are your servants." There is no philosophically or spiritually neutral subject matter.

Fall

The universality of Creation is matched by the universality of the Fall. The Bible teaches that all parts of creation—including our minds—are caught up in a great rebellion against the Creator. Theologians call this the "noetic" effect of the Fall (the effect on the mind), and it subverts our ability to understand the world apart from God's regenerating grace.

Of course, nonbelievers still function in God's world, bear God's image, and are upheld by God's common grace, which means they are capable of uncovering isolated segments of genuine knowledge. And Christians should welcome those insights. All truth is God's truth. Nevertheless, the overall systems of thought constructed by nonbelievers will be false—for if the system is not built on biblical truth, then it will be built on some other ultimate principle. A Christian approach to any field needs to be both critical and constructive. We cannot simply borrow from the results of secular scholarship as though that were spiritually neutral territory discovered by people whose minds are completely open and objective—that is, as though the Fall had never happened.

Redemption

Finally, Redemption is as comprehensive as Creation and Fall. God does not save only our souls, while leaving our minds to function on their own. He redeems the whole person. Conversion is meant

> Our calling is not just to "get to heaven" but also to cultivate the earth, not just to "save souls" but also to serve God through our work.

to give new direction to our thoughts, emotions, will, and habits. Paul urges us to offer up our entire selves to God as "living sacrifices," so that we will not be "conformed to this world" but be "transformed by the renewal of [our] minds" (Rom. 12:1-2). When we are redeemed, all things are made new (2 Cor. 5:17).

Redemption consists primarily in casting out our mental idols and turning back to the true God. And when we do that, we will experience His transforming power renewing every aspect of our lives. To talk about a Christian worldview is simply another way of saying that when we are redeemed, our entire outlook on life is re-centered on God and re-built on His revealed truth.

READ THE DIRECTIONS:
The Cultural Mandate

How do we go about constructing a Christian worldview? The key passage is the creation account in Genesis, because that's where we are taken back to the beginning to learn what God's original purpose was in creating the human race. With the entrance of sin, humans went off course, lost their way, wandered off the path. But when we accept Christ's salvation, we are put back on the right path and are restored to our original purpose. Redemption is not just about being saved from sin, it is also about being saved to

something—to resume the task for which we were originally created.

And what was that task? In Genesis, God gives what we might call the first job description: "Be fruitful and multiply and fill the earth and subdue it." The first phrase, "be fruitful and multiply," means to develop the social world: build families, churches, schools, cities, governments, laws. The second phrase, "subdue the earth," means to harness the natural world: plant crops, build bridges, design computers, compose music. This passage is sometimes called the Cultural Mandate because it tells us that our original purpose was to create cultures, build civilizations—nothing less.[2]

This means that our vocation or professional work is not a second-class activity, something we do just to put food on the table. It is the high calling for which we were originally created. The way we serve a Creator God is by being creative with the talents and gifts He has given us. We could even say that we are called to continue God's own creative work.

In the first six days of the Genesis narrative, God forms then fills the physical universe. Then the narrative pauses, as though to emphasize that the next step will be the culmination of all that has gone before. This is the only stage in the

creative process when God announces His plan ahead of time, when the members of the Trinity consult with one another: Let Us make a creature in Our image, who will represent Us and carry on Our work on earth (see Gen. 1:26). Then God creates the first human couple, to have dominion over the earth and govern it in His name.

It is obvious from the text that humans are not supreme rulers, autonomously free to do whatever they wish. Their dominion is a delegated authority: They are representatives of the Supreme Ruler, called to reflect His holy and loving care for creation. They are to "cultivate" the earth—a word that has the same root as "culture." The way we express the image of God is by being creative and building cultures.

This was God's purpose when He originally created human beings, and it remains His purpose for us today. God's original plan was not abrogated by the Fall. Sin has corrupted every aspect of human nature, but it has not made us less than human. We still reflect, "through a glass, darkly" (1 Cor. 13:12 KJV), our original nature as God's image-bearers. Even nonbelievers carry out the Cultural Mandate: They "multiply and fill the earth"—which is to say, they get married, raise families, start schools, run businesses. And they "cultivate the

How many do the hard work of crafting real answers to the questions they are raising? How many cry out to God on behalf of people struggling in the coils of false worldviews?

earth"—they fix cars, write books, study nature, invent new gadgets.

After I spoke at a conference, a young woman said to me, "When you talk about the Cultural Mandate, you're not talking about anything distinctively Christian; these are things everybody does." But that's precisely the point: Genesis is telling us our true nature, the things we can't help doing, the way God created everyone to function. Our purpose is precisely to fulfill our God-given nature.

The Fall did not destroy our original calling, but only made it more difficult. Our work is now marked by sorrow and hard labor. In Genesis 3:16 and 17, the Hebrew uses the same word for the "labor" of childbearing and the "labor" of growing food. The text suggests that the two central tasks of adulthood—raising the next generation and making a living—will be fraught with the pain of living in a fallen and fractured world. All our efforts will be twisted and misdirected by sin and selfishness.

Yet when God redeems us, He releases us from the guilt and power of sin and restores us to our full humanity, so that we can once again carry out the tasks for which we were created. Because of Christ's redemption on the cross, our work takes on a new aspect as well—it becomes a means of sharing in His redemptive purposes. In cultivating creation, we not only recover our original purpose but also bring a redemptive force to reverse the evil and corruption introduced by the Fall. With hearts and minds renewed, our work can now be inspired by love for God and delight in His service.

The lesson of the Cultural Mandate is that our sense of fulfillment depends on engaging in creative, constructive work. The ideal human existence is not eternal leisure or an endless vacation—or even a monastic retreat into prayer and meditation—but creative effort expended for the glory of God and the benefit of others. Our calling is not just to "get to heaven" but also to cultivate the earth, not just to "save souls" but also to serve God through our work. For God Himself is engaged not only in the work of salvation (special grace) but also in the work of preserving and developing His creation (common grace). When we obey the Cultural Mandate, we participate in the work of God Himself, as agents of His common grace.

Redemption means entering upon a lifelong quest to devote our skills and talents to building things that are beautiful and useful, while fighting the forces of evil and sin that oppress and distort the creation. Some theologians suggest a fourth category should be Glorification, to call to mind our final goal of living in the new heavens and new earth, for which our work here is a preparation. Whatever term we use, being a Christian means embarking on a lifelong process of growth in grace, both in our personal lives (sanctification) and in our vocations (cultural renewal).

BORN TO GROW UP:
Our Personal Role

Each of us has a role to play in cultivating the creation and working out God's norms for a just and humane society. By sheer necessity, of course, a large percentage of our time is devoted to running businesses, teaching schools, publishing newspapers, playing in orchestras, and everything else needed to keep a civilization thriving. Even those who work in "full-time Christian service" still need to clean the house, take care of the kids, and mow the lawn. It is imperative for us to understand that in carrying out these tasks, we are not doing inferior or second-tier work for the Kingdom. Instead we are agents of God's common grace, doing His work in the world.

By God's grace, we can make a significant difference within our sphere of influence—but only as we "crucify" our craving for success, power, and public acclaim. "If anyone would come after me," Jesus said, "let him deny himself and take up his cross daily and follow me" (Luke 9:23). If we long to be given the mind of Christ, we must first be willing to submit to the pattern of suffering He modeled for us. We should expect the process of developing a Christian worldview to be a difficult and painful struggle—first inwardly, as we uproot the idols in our own thought life, and then outwardly, as we face the hostility of a fallen and unbelieving world. Our strength for the task must come from spiritual union with Christ, recognizing that suffering is the route to being conformed to Him and remade into His image.

GOD WINS:
Applying a
Christian Worldview

Once we discover that the Christian worldview is really true, then living it out means offering up to God all our powers—practical, intellectual, emotional, artistic—to live for Him in every area of life. The only expression such faith can take is one that captures our entire being and redirects our every thought. The notion of a secular/sacred split becomes unthinkable. Biblical truth takes hold of our inner being, and we recognize that it is not only a message of salvation but also the truth about all reality. God's Word becomes a light to all our paths, providing the foundational principles for bringing every part of our lives under the Lordship of Christ, to glorify Him and to cultivate His creation.

After becoming a Christian, I discovered how liberating a worldview approach can be. There is no need to avoid the secular world and hide out behind the walls of an evangelical subculture; instead, Christians can appreciate works of art and culture as products of human creativity expressing the image of God. On the other hand, there is no danger of being naive or uncritical about false and dangerous messages embedded in secular culture, because a worldview gives the conceptual tools needed to analyze and critique them. Believers can apply a distinctively biblical perspective every time they pick up the newspaper, watch a movie, or read a book.

IN LOVE WITH
CREATIVITY:
Creating Culture

Our first response to the great works of human culture—whether in art or technology or economic productivity—should be to celebrate them as reflections of God's own creativity. And even when we analyze where they go wrong, it should be in a spirit of love. Today on religious radio or in ministry fund-raising letters, it is common for Christian activists to attack Hollywood or television or rap music in tones of aggrieved anger, berating their immoral content or mocking the pretensions of postmodern political correctness. Today, Christian activists are quick to organize a boycott or pressure a politician to de-fund some artistic group, and these strategies have their place. But how many reach out to the artists with compassion? How many do the hard work of crafting real answers to the questions they are raising? How many cry out to God on behalf of people struggling in the coils of false worldviews?

Christians need to move beyond criticizing culture to creating culture. That is the task God originally created humans to do, and in the process of sanctification we are meant to recover that task. Whether we work with our brains or with our hands, whether we are analytical or artistic, whether we work with people or with things, in every calling we are culture-creators, offering up our work as service to God. **C**

---

1. Clouser, Myth of Religious Neutrality, 80.
2. When I lecture on the Cultural Mandate, many people say that they have never encountered the concept before. Thus readers may benefit from my more detailed treatment of the Cultural Mandate in "Saved to What?" chapter 31 in How Now Shall we Live?

Nancy Randolph Pearcey is the Francis A. Schaeffer Scholar at the World Journalism Institute, where Total Truth serves as the basis for a worldview curriculum. A former, agnostic, she earned M.A. from Covenant Theological Seminary. Currently she serves as a Visiting Scholar at the Torrey Honors Institute at Biola University, and a Senior Fellow at the Discovery Institute. Pearcey has authored or contributed to several works, including the ECPA Gold Medallion winner How Now Shall We Live? and Crossway's The Soul of Science.

Before the Latch Broke or A Return to the Way Things Were

SEEING THE GOSPEL IN GARDEN STATE

By Jason Locy

DAVID JENKINS. THIS IS A GUY I WENT TO HIGH SCHOOL WITH WHO BECAME A COP. ALTHOUGH I NEVER SAW HIM DO COKE LINES OFF A URINAL, HE DID THREATEN TO KILL A TEACHER ONE TIME. ALAN THOMPSON. THIS IS A KID I KNEW WHO WORKED AT THE AIRPORT AND STOLE PEOPLE'S LUGGAGE AND THEN SOLD IT OUT OF THE BACK OF HIS CAR. NOT QUITE LIKE STEALING STUFF FROM DEAD PEOPLE, BUT STILL A PRETTY MEAN THING TO DO. AND, ALTHOUGH I WAS NEVER FRIENDS WITH ANYONE WHO PUSHED HIS MOM INTO THE KITCHEN COUNTER WHEN HE WAS NINE, PARALYZING HER FROM THE WAIST DOWN THUS PROMPTING HIS PSYCHIATRIST DAD TO MEDICATE HIM OUT OF HIS MIND FOR THE NEXT 17 YEARS, I DID KNOW A HANDFUL OF GUYS THAT WENT THROUGH HIGH SCHOOL AND COLLEGE STONED TRYING TO ESCAPE REALITY.

Because we all have friends that never quite did anything after high school (or became cops, or made lots of money, or are on Prozac), our generation can relate, in one way or another, to all the characters in writer/director/actor Zach Braff's 2004 film, *Garden State*.

As Christians, we can relate to *Garden State* in another way: it tells the Gospel story – a story of hope, love, and forgiveness that is so universal that we see it re-told all around us in countless real life stories, art, and nature. It is a full and ongoing story of the way things once were (creation), the way things are (our fallen state as a result of sin), the way things could be (redemption through Christ), and the way things will be (restoration of all things).

The Gospel story starts at the beginning of time - before Eve ate the fruit, before high cholesterol, before cargo pants for men - when God set things up to operate a certain way. God's creation and intended order for things were perfect. There was no hunger or disease or war. The earth wasn't warming, and there were no hurricanes or tsunamis. Man was in direct communion with Him, and every living thing was experiencing God's creation in all its beauty.

In *Garden State*, there was a time when Braff's character, Large, had a normal life. Like the Gospel story, a better time existed before this story begins. Large was a typical nine-year-old boy with no need for heavy doses of mind numbing medications. His mom wasn't paralyzed and living life in a wheelchair. He had a relationship with his dad and mom and crazy aunts and uncles. He felt things like anger, happiness, and love.

But then Large pushed his mom, and because a quarter inch piece of plastic that latched the dishwasher shut was broken, she fell and become paralyzed. With this one moment, this one decision to act out, things changed. Now, all the things that were right and normal in Large's life begin to suffer. His mom isn't healthy and walking, he is on of all sorts of prescription medication, he can no longer feel, and he hasn't seen his family in nine years.

In the Gospel story, a latch didn't break on a dishwasher; rather, man decided we could do things better than God and chose to try things our own way. With this one decision, something happened and creation was no longer the way God intended it to be. Instead, everything is all messed up and broken and not working properly. As a result we are stuck here on an earth that isn't really functioning the way it is supposed to.

In the opening scene of the film, we see a great illustration of Large's current situation. He is sitting on a plane that is crashing. Everyone around him screaming for their lives, horrified, knowing they will die in just a matter of moments. Large sits in his seat calmly, staring ahead, moving only to adjust the airflow from the control above his head. Then, the controls above his head turn into a ringing phone and we realize, as the ringing phone awakens him, that he is just dreaming.

Large is numb, catatonic. He doesn't feel anything or care about anyone. He doesn't cry, and he is estranged from his family. Like the Gospel story, Large is living a life that is far different from when things first started.

When Large's mom dies, he returns home to New Jersey for her funeral, purposefully leaving his medications in L.A. He begins to realize that he is missing out on life--that the life he is currently living is so screwed up and so far off course from how it started, he needs to stop his medication and figure it all out. And that's the thing about the Gospel story. It doesn't just stop once things get all messed up and we are eternally screwed up.

Instead, God sent His Son and now things can be different.

Because of the death and resurrection of Jesus, there is hope. Through His death we see that things can be better again. Life can get back to the way it once was, and we can work to reverse the effects of the fall. Even though we may never experience it here on earth, there is hope that one day things will be back to the way He intended them to be.

Towards the beginning of the film, there is a scene where Large is at a party with his old high school friends and everyone is high on Ecstasy and playing Spin the Bottle. The bottle lands on Large and a girl in the room gives him a long, passionate kiss. In the director's commentary, Braff describes this kiss as "kinda defibrillating" Large out of his numbness. And, even though Large is high on Ecstasy, he is off his medication for the first time in a very long time, and this is the beginning of him feeling things again. He realizes what he has probably expected all along - that things could and should be different.

The morning after the party, he meets Sam (Natalie Portman) and the rest of the film is a beautiful story of love and hope as Large begins a journey to experience life without his medication. Like our story, Large is trying to make things better. He is working towards feeling again, towards loving, and towards making things okay with his dad. He realizes things may not ever be the same but he also knows he has to try.

Like Large, we journey through life trying to make things as good as they can be. We realize that there may never be a cure for AIDS, and that there may always be poverty and injustices around the globe, but we try to stop it anyway. We try our best to put things back the way God intended them to be.

Although we may not ever experience things as they were intended, it is still our job to try to make things right here on earth. The great thing, though, is that one day we will see things the way God made them. We will see earth in all of its beauty. Relationships, lives, and creation will be restored back to their created state.

This happens in *Garden State* as Large's life begins to return to the way it was before his mom's accident and before all his medication. His feelings and emotions return as he falls in love with Sam. He talks to his father. He sheds a tear for the first time in a long time, and, in a burst of emotions, he yells off the top of a crane into an endless abyss.

Garden State ends with the hope that things will return to the way they once were and Large's life will somehow be better. The Gospel story ends in the same way as all things are made new again and things are returned to their intended state.

As we begin to engage the culture around us we see the Gospel story re-told over and over again. That's the beauty of our story; we can see it everywhere and in everything. **C**

Jason Locy is Creative Director at FiveStone. Jason and his wife Heather live in Atlanta with their two boys, Ethan and Christian. Ethan would like a dog but Jason said no. Email him at **jasonlocy@fivestone.com**.

BY TIM WILLARD

MYTHS OF ENGAGEMENT

ADMIT IT. THE IDEA OF ENGAGING CULTURE IS INTIMIDATING. THERE ARE SO MANY QUESTIONS AND FEARS.

"How can I be Salt and Light?"
"Will I fall into the traps of the world?"
"I am just not a trendy leader."

How can we pursue and engage culture when we are bound up and paralyzed by these concerns? What would happen if we allowed truth to shine through our fears, exposing the myths culture throws at us for what they really are? We would be empowered with renewed confidence to step into the ring and engage culture. Let's dispel a few of these Myths of Cultural Engagement.

Myth #1 - *My method(s) of engagement must be flashy to be effective.*

We are often fooled into the belief that only churches who host stadium-sized conferences, big name speakers, concert-style worship, or local television programs can make a great impact. While there is value in presenting a message to the masses, the church doesn't have to be huge to make a huge impact. Through personal experience I have found creating a flashy or entertaining event usually entails a huge budget and much stress.

Truth – *Effectively engaging culture requires Christian leaders to be authentic.*

For three years my friends and I toured the country in a used van, playing music for youth groups, college groups, churches, pubs, book stores, coffee shops and festivals. Our band consisted of a girl on cello, a guy on acoustic guitar, and me. Obviously, our sound didn't blow down any doors. Our goal was to present crowds (regardless of how many) with an authentic musical experience that communicated our hearts and led them to a deeper experience musically and spiritually. We shared our lives from stage, and were passionate about what we were doing. After each show, we took time to talk with the youth and adults, allowing God to use not just the music, but also our individual lives to touch people's hearts.

What transpired at our concerts was very humbling. Many times the music was used as the tipping point for an individual spiritual awakening, or even congregational healing. It was beautiful to be a part of.

Engage

The beauty of our ministry came not from the spectacular, but from the authentic. We were whom God made us to be, flaws and all. Vulnerability is extremely rewarding in terms of seeing your life used by God to touch others. We must be open and willing to let people inside before true intimacy can take root. Remember, bigger is not always better. Authentic Christian love is just as startling as a huge event planned with all the bells and whistles. What does your church (and its leaders) do to cultivate authentic relationships? How do you communicate and live out authenticity personally?

Myth #2 – *We must have top—notch programming at our church to effectively engage our culture.*

No disrespect to programs – programs do have their place. Programs come in many different methods, forms, and titles. The problem comes when programs trap leaders. Some churches or organizations rely on high profile, highly structured programs to attract and engage outsiders and unbelievers. The success of a program is more easily measured in numbers than life change, which is harder to compartmentalize. A program may run for years without anyone stopping to ask whether or not it is actually effective.

Truth – *Programs are stale. Our culture thirsts for intimacy.*

The tide has changed in evangelicalism. The truth is people in culture are less interested in a church programs as they are in whether or not they will be accepted, cared for and loved. If the outside world observes Believers in churches loving one another, living what they preach and being vulnerable, then effective engagement comes naturally.

Engage

Friends of mine lead in churches that use small groups and family-centered worship experiences as an intimate and highly effective approach to engaging culture. What are some "sacred cow" programs at your church? Do they foster a sense of intimacy? How can you create intimate environments for all people to connect with God and each other?

Myth #3– *As long as I keep up with current trends socially, spiritually and mentally then that is good enough.*

Though Paul writes in Romans 12:2, "Do not conform to the patterns of this world," even Christ-followers fall into the common lie that says you must look a certain way to be "cool." Despite the fact that the new age in history affords us the ability to be ourselves, we still try to look and act like whatever is most popular in culture. How does that express authenticity?

The second part of this verse talks about being transformed by the renewing of your mind. Inward change is the source of authenticity. It begins with our minds.

Christ Followers are often seen as anti-intellectuals ... we don't want to think deeply or consider new ideas because we have all the answers. We have successfully created a sub-culture, with our own brands of music, film, and books. By having "Christian" everything we cease to engage culture. The pursuit for excellence is no longer important. We are happy with our music, books and film even if some of them are sub-par. This breeds mediocrity.

Think about some of the great Christian influencers of the past century: C.S. Lewis, Francis Schaeffer, G.K. Chesterton, and J.R.R. Tolkein. These timeless leaders were not content to create the typical. They forged ahead with new ideas and creativity that still shapes our culture! The excellence of their craft transcended culture, both Christian and mainstream.

Truth – *Trends fade and image is nothing. Timeless truths apply to all generations.*

Vintage never goes out of style. It only gains credibility with time. Think of your faith as being "vintage." Christ-followers believe in timeless truths that relate to every person on earth. It is time we assert our theology to culture, not in a legalistic manner, but as the foundation we build our lives on. Trends and fads in culture are based on elements of a time era. Out Truth transcends time.

Engage

Engaging culture does not mean to "go with the flow;" rather, it implies active participation. A leader is a reader. Become familiar with culture and understand the context of our story by reading about history, artists, educators and philosophers. Do not compromise your intellect for the sake of relevance.

If you want to focus on image, focus on this: God created human beings in His image. You are God's "workmanship." This word in Ephesians 2:10 can also be rendered "poem." You are the creative output of a God who found great pleasure in making you unique. There is no special formula to help you become "in" with culture. We hear very little of Christ and his cool band of suave disciples. They were ruffians, vagabonds, social castaways, and fisherman and chances are they were not pre-occupied with their robes or tunics. Do yourself a favor—be you. **C**

Tim Willard is a freelance writer and speaker from Lititz, Pennsylvania. He has B.S. in Bible and is currently pursuing his Master's in Theological Studies at Wheaton College. You can check out Tim and his wife Chris' passion for ministry, writing, and all things beautiful at **www.flickernail.com**. Tim exclusively rides Kona mountain bikes.

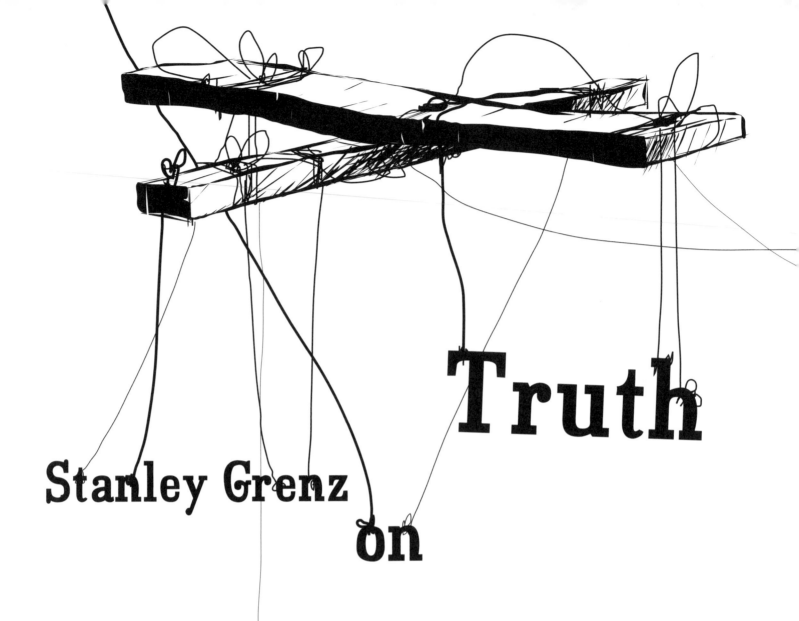

Truth

Stanley Grenz on

AT HIS TRIAL BEFORE PILATE, JESUS DECLARED THAT HE HAD COME INTO THE WORLD TO TESTIFY TO THE TRUTH. "WHAT IS TRUTH?" THE CYNICAL ROMAN GOVERNOR ASKED RHETORICALLY IN RESPONSE.

(JOHN 18:37-38)

Many people, especially those educated before the 1970s, might well dismiss Pilate's wistful words as the outmoded machinations of a premodern skeptic. They likely would direct the governor to modern scientific advances that, in their estimation, have discovered a host of truths about the world that were unknown in the first century. Yet, just when the scientific understanding of truth seemed to have attained undisputed sovereignty, Pilate's haunting query, *"What is Truth?"* has re-emerged with a vengeance.

Participatory Truth

Contrary to what some commentators suggest, postmoderns have not dismissed truth. On the contrary, like people in every era, they, too, are on a quest for truth. Nevertheless, postmoderns tend to operate from a conception of truth that differs from the reigning modern view.

The modern era was born when certain philosophers concluded that truth is a characteristic of true statements, and a statement is true if it declares what is in fact the case. Paralleling this conception

of truth is an assumption that the world operates according to universal laws. Although these "laws of nature" function independently of the human mind, Enlightenment thinkers theorized that such laws nevertheless can be discerned by human reason. Consequently, the truth (or falsity) of any particular statement may be readily determined, at least in theory, merely by comparing it with the dimension of the world that it purports to describe. An assertion is true, therefore, if it represents accurately or describes correctly a specific facet or detail of the

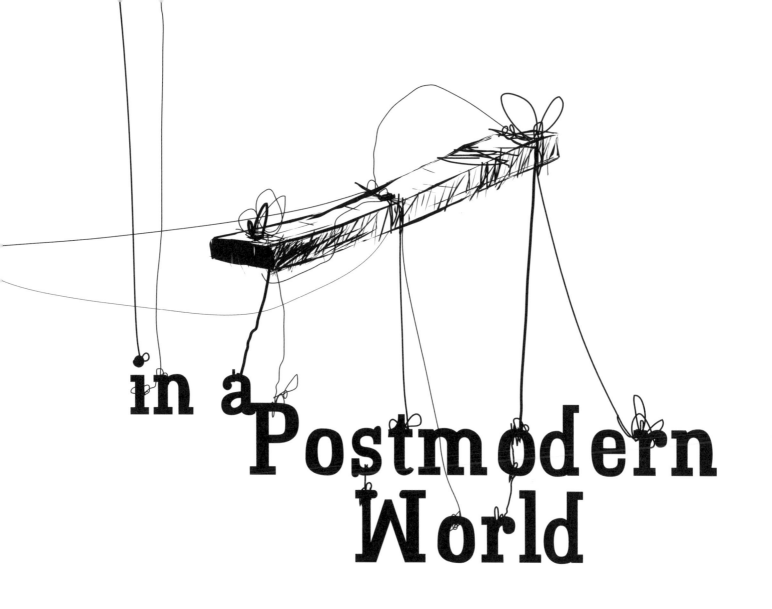

in a Postmodern World

world. So, according to the modern concept of truth, the sentence *"Snow is white"* is true if snow is indeed white. And we can determine the truth of the statement simply by inspecting snow to determine its color.

Most of us go about our day-to-day routine operating on such assumptions. Enlightenment thinkers, however, took the matter a step further and extended without end the boundaries of what human reason could supposedly fathom. In so doing they held out hope that human scientific discovery eventually could devise the one true and complete description of the world as it really is. And in so doing, they hoped to inaugurate the utopian society.

The postmodernist questions these central assumptions of the modern outlook. According to postmoderns, truth is not merely a quality of statements that ascribe properties to the world. Nor should truth be limited to what can be verified by reason and the empirical scientific method. Instead, postmoderns are convinced that there are ways of knowing in addition to reason, such as through the emotions and the intuition. And, rather than as a realm of impersonal laws, postmoderns view the world as historical, relational, personal and participatory.

Postmoderns, therefore, would answer Pilate's question by inviting him to participate in the truth. Pilate never will come to know that Jesus is the Christ unless he takes the step of participating

in what Jesus embodies. To know the truth, he must respond personally to the Master's invitation, "Come and see." Postmoderns might also urge Pilate to realize that the discovery of truth involves him as a whole person. It must grab his emotions and stir his intuition, as well as satisfy his reason. The pathway to knowing involves all these dimensions simultaneously. For this reason, Pilate should, for example, take seriously his wife's disconcerting dream, realizing that she may well have gained through intuition what his intellectual cynicism prohibited him from accepting.

Constructed Truth
Enlightenment thinkers argued that the pursuit of truth requires that we stand apart from what we are observing. We

to view the world from a neutral vantage point "above" the world.

Postmoderns deny that we enjoy such an Archimedean vantage point – a "view from nowhere" – from which to gain a purely objective view of reality "out there." Not only is the world participatory, they aver, we structure or construct the world we experience through the concepts we bring to it. Hence, all the words we use to describe the world, including even such seemingly empirical terms as *snow* and *white*, do not denote or describe realities that actually exist "out there." Rather, our language consists of a set of social conventions or agreed upon human constructs that allow us to experience the world in a particular manner.

Some postmoderns go so far as to claim that we do not inhabit a single objective world as such, for different people live in the particular worlds they create. Consequently, they add, there is no final basis for determining truth, no "real world" against which we can adjudicate in some final, objective fashion among the variety of linguistic worlds that various groups of people create. As a result, many postmoderns are content to allow seemingly conflicting constructions of reality to exist side by side.

In the modern era, the realm constructed by appeal to the language of empirical science was believed to be the only truly real world. And scientific knowledge, with its appeal to neutral, objective "facts" obtained by means of dispassionate, disconnected observation, was the sole claimant to the lofty designation "truth." Whatever else it may be, postmodernism is the questioning of this narrowing of the concept of truth to the sphere of empirical science.

Postmoderns, therefore, might respond to Pilate by suggesting that his cultural training as a Roman has disposed him to view religious claims in the cynical manner that characterized his response to Jesus. But the man standing before him offered the Roman governor a new framework, a new set of lenses through which to see himself, an entirely different set of categories that comprised a glorious new world in which he could have lived. Jesus' invitation to him, therefore, was, "Change worlds!"

Narrative Truth
Truth is connected to narratives. Because the modern understanding of truth is closely related to the belief that the world operates according to knowable, universal laws, the modern quest for truth entails a search for the unchanging principles that lie behind the changing data of life. Consequently, moderns generally view stories

Postmoderns are impressed less with well-reasoned arguments that supposedly prove the rightness of our claims to truth than with the life of a truth-embodying community.

as merely illustrative. Narratives are at best illustrations of abiding principles. And after we have discovered the abiding principles that a particular narrative illustrates, we can discard the story. Postmoderns, in contrast, see an integral connection between story and truth. Truth is lived narrative. And the goal of storytelling is not simply to extract the truth that it supposedly illustrates, but to "inhabit" the story.

Consider the request of James and John for prominent places in their Lord's coming kingdom. (Mark 10:32-45) In approaching this text, the modern exegete or preacher typically seeks to dissect the story in search of the timeless principle for which the narrative is an illustration. The modern thinker is interested in answering questions such as, What universal, transcultural "truth" was Jesus seeking to convey to his disciples? Or what point does Mark want his readers to gain from the story? These questions treat the text as a pointer to a deeper "truth," rather than as being the truth itself.

For the postmodern, the truth of the story does not lie in the principles that it supposedly embodies, but in the story itself. Truth emerges as the hearers are drawn into the narrative, as they become James and John, and hence as they hear their Lord admonishing them as well.

The narrative character of truth may also be seen by appeal to participation in the sacraments or ordinances of the church. Debates regarding the "real presence" of Jesus in the Eucharist, which have agitated theologians at least since the 16th century, have their place, of course. Yet, viewed from a postmodern perspective, the power of these celebrations does not lie in attempts to describe whether and how being baptized or communing at the Lord's table mediates divine grace to our lives. Rather, baptism and the Lord's Supper are enacted narratives. The goal of these community rites is to lead us to participate anew in the story of Jesus in this symbolic manner. And this participation, in turn, emboldens us to participate in that story in our day-in and day-out living as well.

The postmodern might well respond to Pilate, therefore, by telling him the old, old story of Jesus and His love. In so doing, the apologist becomes an evangelist. The telling of the narrative comprises an invitation to the cynical Roman governor to forsake the narrative inculcated in him by his pagan, imperial overlord and participate in the glorious narrative of God at work in Christ reconciling the world to Himself.

Pragmatic Truth

The idea that we construct the world through the social conventions we bring to it leads to a decisively communal understanding of truth. Postmoderns declare that not only the specific truths we accept but even our understanding of truth are a function of the social group – the community – in which we participate. Truth is what fits within a specific community; truth exists in the ground rules that facilitate the well-being of a community.

The communal nature of truth results in a new kind of relativism, precipitated by life in social groups – or tribes – each of which has its own language, beliefs and values. The older, individualistic relativism elevated personal choice as the "be all" and "end all." Its maxims were: "Each to his own" and "Everyone has a right to her own opinion." Postmoderns, in contrast, espouse a communal relativism, expressed in maxims such as, "What is right for us may not be right for you" and "What is wrong in our context may in your context be okay or even preferable."

This postmodern situation was capsulated in an episode of *Star Trek: The Next Generation* ("Ethics") that aired several years ago. An accident has robbed Lt. Worf of the use of his legs. In Klingon society, this means he is as good as dead. Therefore, in keeping with his own cultural mores, Worf plans to end his life, and he asks his good friend, Will Riker, to assist him in the death ritual. Loath to participate in such a despicable act, Riker goes to the ship's captain, Jean-Luc Picard, for advice. Rather than invoking any individualistic or objectivist concept of absolute and universal right and wrong, Picard appeals to Riker to realize that what from his cultural perspective might appear to be an act of suicide, when viewed according to the mores of Klingon society, is perfectly permissible, even necessary. He then concludes his remarks by counselling Riker to make his decision on the basis of the fact that Worf is looking to him as a trusted friend.

Here again, the participatory understanding of truth emerges. For the postmodern, Pilate's question can be answered only within a particular social context. Viewed from this perspective, truth is not exhausted by indubitable facts that ascribe qualities to the world. Instead, truth is active. Truth is what accomplishes a goal. Truth is what "works." Truth is what creates a community of truth in which truth comes to expression in the relationships shared by the members of the group.

This aspect of the postmodern understanding of truth provides the great opportunity and the great challenge to followers of Jesus. Postmoderns are impressed less with well-reasoned arguments that supposedly prove the rightness of our claims to truth than with the life of a truth-embodying community. Consequently, when viewed from a postmodern perspective, the final answer to Pilate's question lies in the fellowship of the disciples who live in the light of the resurrection of the crucified Jesus by the power of the outpoured Holy Spirit. As I have heard said repeatedly in recent years, postmoderns are converted to community before they are converted to Christ. But then, this ought not come as a surprise. For Jesus himself declared, "By this all will know that you are my disciples, if you love one another." (John 13:35 NKJV) And love for one another as those who love God and are loved by God is the ultimate description of the kind of truth that, when known, sets us free. (John 8:32). **C**

Adapted from the article "Answering Pilate," which appeared in The Life@Work Journal *March/April 2001. Used by permission of Life@Work.*

The late **Stanley J. Grenz** was a leading evangelical scholar. Based in Vancouver, Canada's Carey Theological College and Mars Hill Graduate School in Seattle WA, Dr. Grenz wrote prolifically and lectured throughout the world. His books include *A Primer on Postmodernism* and *What Christians Really Believe & Why*. He is survived by his wife, Edna and two adult children.

Book Review

with special tribute from michael w. smith

roaring lambs

a gentle plan to
radically change
your world

Bob Briner

TITLE:
Roaring Lambs
AUTHOR: Bob Briner

REVIEW BY: Melissa Kruse

Do Christian values belong in our culture? The late Bob Briner would have told you, "Absolutely!" In his book, *Roaring Lambs*, Briner issues a wake up call to those of us who are sitting on the sidelines of our faith. As "salt and light" of the earth, we have a responsibility to fulfill the cultural mandate. This is a book about strategy—using our voice as Christians to create social change and make an impact in our workplace and in the world.

Briner asks the question, "Who speaks for Christians?" To be a roaring lamb means that we are actively involved in dialogue and decisions on social and political issues that impact the quality of life in our workplace and communities. He believes the most effective spokesperson for Jesus Christ in the public arena will not be the televangelist or big-name Christian author, speaker, or artist. Rather, it is the informed citizen who engages their community in dialogue; the workplace leaders who build relationships with their peers; and the gifted Christian writers, speakers, and artists who win print space and airtime in the American mainstream through their competence and class in their "secular" profession ... "earning the right to be heard."

As leaders, how can we expect to engage the world if we are not familiar with the things within it? To better engage and influence those around us, we must submerge ourselves in the culture and environment. There are important roles for us to fulfill in education, politics, art, and the media. Rather than protesting, we should be proclaiming. If our desire is to be an agent of change, we must not only challenge the status quo, but also provide alternatives and solutions to impact our world.

Having recently graduated from college, I am concerned about how to balance my career (the world) and my faith. Reading this book helped me realize that I cannot separate who I am from the things I do. Being a roaring lamb is less about "balance" and more about integration. Briner tells us that we must openly be who we are, integrating our Christian faith into our daily lives. Knowing and loving God's word, and choosing to integrate it in relevant, articulate, convincing, and good-natured ways, earns us the right to be heard. Though at times it will be challenging, we can be everyday people, doing everyday jobs and still be roaring lambs for our Shepherd. **C**

ROARING LAMB QUIZ

How loud do you roar?

While we do not usually think of lambs as strong and assertive creatures, under the guidance of a shepherd they trust, they are fearless. We too have a Shepherd in which we can live strong and secure. We must be roaring lambs for Christ and His Kingdom.

Take the following test by answering each statement yes or no, then check your score at the end.

1. I have attended a school board meeting within the last year.

2. I have as many close friends outside the church as within.

3. I own at least one original piece of art.

4. In the last year I have written a letter of praise to a network or sponsor of a television program.

5. I support decent movies by attending wholesome ones and avoiding unwhole some ones.

6. I consider careers in the arts, journalism, literature, film, and television to be as important for the kingdom as pastoral ministry or foreign missions.

7. I have written at least one letter to the editor of my local newspaper in the last year.

8. I have read at least one book on the New Your Times Bestseller List in the past year.

9. I am active in the civic affairs of my community.

10. I have talked with at least one non-Christian about my relationship with Christ and what it means to be His follower.

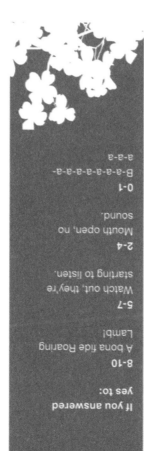

If you answered yes to:

8-10
A bona fide Roaring Lamb!

5-7
Watch out, they're starting to listen.

2-4
Mouth open, no sound.

0-1
B-a-a-a-a-a-a-a-a-a

Journal

What does ENGAGED IN CULTURE mean to me?

THINK

Applying L3
Gaining Wisdom Through Life Long Learning

BY DR. RON MARTOIA

If Solomon is the wisest man of all, and if wisdom is knowledge applied, then apparently Solomon was acquiring vast amounts of information and knowledge. Let's be reminded it was he who said that knowledge was power and strength. (Proverbs 24:3-6)

There are four types of people walking around on the planet, back in 1050 A.D. Salomon Ibn Gabirol identified them.

*1. There are those that know not and know not they know not;
they are fools – shun them.*

*2. There are those that know not and know they know not;
they are simple – teach them.*

*3. There are those who know and know not they know;
they are asleep – awaken them.*

*4. There are those that know and know that they know;
they are wise – follow them.*

Now when it comes to leadership I am going to make a counterintuitive observation about the preceding four statements. Leadership is essentially about constantly embracing number two so we can consistently move toward number four.

When leaders become learn-ed they become useless because the shelf life on learning is increasingly small. But when leaders move from being learn-ed to being learners we are on the path of adventure.

Let me give you a couple reasons why learning is so critical.

First, I hope you share with me a DNA level assumption; the best ways of leading, of doing ministry, of reaching people, of developing Christ-followers have yet to be discovered. I genuinely believe that. Learning is the palette used to mix the new colors of those new ways.

Second, the incarnation of Jesus requires a deep commitment to Life Long Learning. We have a very complex task as leaders; take an ancient, ever relevant and necessary message, and translate it into a shifting changing culture so the people in that culture understand and "get it." That means we not only have to be biblical experts, (that is the ancient message part) but we also have to be very creative, delicate and informed (that is the translation part), and we have to be culturally adept, in tune, and aware so our translation connects (that is the "gets it" part). And in the midst of all that work we are attempting to cast vision, inspire and align our communities to make all this happen incarnationally. Sounds to me like a need for learning.

Third, what is the one thing underlying all change? What is the one foundation of all growth? What is the one assumption made of every Christian Leader? The answer is revealed in the one word Jesus used of every follower, he called them mathetes or quite literally learners, we usually translate it disciple. Jesus expects you and I as followers, let alone as leaders of others to be learning and growing.

To be a disciple is to be a learner, to be a leader who is a disciple is to make a commitment to put your learning on steroids.

While learning isn't just taking in information it does have to start there, and it is on this information intake that we are going to focus.

What I would like to do is help you construct a customized plan that will serve you forever. I know sounds audacious, but honestly, it can be done.

These are the key questions in constructing this plan.

Plan Construction Question #1
What areas of learning, if you were to stay on top of, would significantly impact, feed and source your life and leadership development?

Great question and not easily answered. Take some time to start capturing those areas.

For me I realized I had to read in a dozen areas with regularity and consistency if I was going to stay at the top of my leadership game and if I was going to be a thought leader in the areas of my unique gifting.

I have had a habit now for nearly two decades to read in the areas of creativity/innovation, leadership, culture, biblical theology, hermeneutics/literary theory, relationships/ emotional intelligence, church ministry models/Missiology, change management/ theory, spiritual formation, health/fitness, and trends.

While there are other areas I read in, those are constantly at the top of the list and I am on a constant look out for the best new resources emerging in those arenas.

Let me invite you to start compiling the list of areas you want to be on the look out for and want to develop in.

Plan Construction Question #2
What is the texture, timing and rhythm of your learning?

Texture

What are the input channels you use? Books are a great source. But what about book reviews? I try and read about 40-50 a month. What about web articles (no need to say things are too expensive, tons of things on the web are free)?

What about MP3 downloads? A new resource I have developed for leaders is a monthly MP3 you can load into computer or iPod and use when you work out or are on the road (**vortexdownload.com**). What about audio books on CD or downloaded? (**audible.com**) and book reviews (**summary.com**)? What about local learning groups? This is one of the biggest trends I see happening all over the country right now as I facilitate 20-25 people in peer to peer learning over a two day round table. Don't forget seminars and conferences, they continue to be a source of learning for thousands of people.

Another layer in the texture of learning is the periodicals and journals you are tapping. I have eight periodicals I monthly subscribe to, from leadership to culture, to theology.

The texture question helps remind us that there are various input channels that make life long learning fun and really quite easy if we just plan ahead and embrace it.

Timing

When do you schedule time for your learning? Notice the question here is not when do you hope you will eventually get to your learning? Wrong question. That one always gets crowded out by things that appear more urgent. Life Long Learning may never feel urgent but it is always important and one of the great antidotes to burn out, tooling exhaustion, and lack of vision.

No, this is a serious question of scheduling. Do you schedule dental appointments? How about medical appointments? Take vitamins daily? Why? Regular check ups and maintenance insure long term health.

I have been blessed with the need for little sleep. So I have always had a habit of early morning reading. In addition to that there are many days that I can also steal and hour in the evening when the rest of the family has hit the rack. Those days I am getting up to three hours of input. This long term discipline is responsible for keeping me fresh in my leadership. It has also enabled me to read 2-3 books a week in addition to the monthly book reviews I try and peruse.

If you let drive time, walking on the treadmill, or when you are getting ready in the morning be a learning time you've just added octane to your leadership life.

Rhythm

While there should be a daily or weekly scheduled block for learning, Life Long Learning is far more than that. Great leaders have always recognized there is a need for a rhythm that allows concentrated, IV-into-the-main-artery-type of learning and reflection that simply can't happen in the typical day to day grind.

Let me make some suggestions that emerge from a rhythm I forged over my nearly 20 year run in a church plant I led. I continue in these to this day and am coaching other point leaders in the same.

Spend a day a month in a Borders or Barnes and Noble. *Yes, the whole day. Goal? Pick an area of the bookstore and bullet hole 20-30 books in the morning. In the afternoon pick another area and do the same. If you don't know how to scan, identify content markers, pick up a copy of How to Read a Book by Adler. This disciple alone radically changed my knowledge base and informed preaching, leadership and developing others.*

Spend two days a quarter off site on a learning retreat. *On that retreat you are taking 3-5 books, audios, mp3, articles, etc ... that you are going to read and reflect on. This is not a prayer retreat though you may pray; it is not a planning retreat though it will no doubt impact your planning. This is a learning retreat, a high octane input retreat.*

Spend 3-5 days annually offsite *(I just did mine with a buddy that I was inviting into my rhythm.) This retreat is a reading, planning, futuring, visioning, time. This is taking all your reading and using it for the express purpose of your leadership development and that of those you lead. I always cover at least one book in three different areas on this retreat; the rest of the time is for vision planning.*

The rhythm question allows us to realize that there are seasons, a time for everything, and that Life Long Learning is something requiring "seasonal" planning.

Construction Planning Question #3
This last question is done at the 3-5 day annual offsite retreat.

Have the Life Long Learning areas I focused on this year served me well? Do they need adjusting? And how have my learning texture, timing and rhythm worked this year?

In short, you are annually evaluating questions #1 and #2 above. This is what keeps your learning fresh through different seasons of life, maturity, ministry and church cycles.

Daniel Boorstin, the incredible writer of intellectual history, says something about all the great inventors, discoverers and innovators in world history, and what he says I think equally applies to leaders.

The biggest barriers to progress in history have not been ignorance but the illusion of knowing.

For us to be genuinely open to learning, we must first embrace our ignorance, admit our need to learn, admit we don't know it all, and willingly and humbly say there is more to learn. When we do that, we open ourselves up to the God of all truth and what he might do in molding and shaping us. And for leaders that is critical, because He must do great things in us before He can do great things through us; which may in fact be the greatest reason to embrace the adventure of Life Long Learning. **C**

Dr. Ron Martoia is a transformational architect ... his passion is helping people, and the organisms they serve, design and experience revolutionary change. Through **Velocityculture.com**, he is using his 20 years of experience on the emerging church landscape to help churches more effectively intersect this native 21st century culture. His most recent endeavor is the launch of **VortexDownload.com**, a monthly downloadable mp3 and .pdf resource for personal and leadership development.

www.injoy.com
Faith-based leadership development in the church and marketplace.

www.christianitytoday.com/leaders
The website of Leadership Journal magazine, with articles, resources, and a free online newsletter subscription.

www.purposedriven.com
Inspired by Rick Warren's vision and books: The Purpose-Driven Church and The Purpose-Driven Life, this website offers daily inspiration and resources for living a purposeful life.

www.relevantmagazine.com
The website of Relevant magazine, with cutting-edge articles and resources for enhancing your Christian walk as you engage the culture.

www.nooma.com
Find here the ten-minute films of Rob Bell, teaching pastor at Mars Hill Bible Church in Grandville, Michigan (www.mhbcmi.org). All "noomas" now come with a thirty-two-page study guide.

www.biblegateway.org
Provides searchable Bibles in various translations, with an exhaustive page of links to other online Christian resources. Includes articles on pop culture and information on the God Blog Conference, which aims to connect Christian bloggers worldwide.

www.creativepastors.com
A ministry of Ed Young, Jr., this site promotes creativity and leadership among pastors by offering resources and sermon series.

www.anewkindofchristian.com
Brian McLaren's website, featuring books, conferences, articles, and an extensive list of recommended reading.

www.ransomedheart.com
Home of Ransomed Heart Ministries, with info on media resources, conferences, retreats, forums, and a newsletter to help you enhance your relationship with Christ.

www.nwma.net
The site of the National Women's Ministry Association, featuring resources and conference information for women leaders.

www.tribalgeneration.com

www.268generation.com

www.allthemore.org

www.bluelikejazz.com

www.blueprintforlife.com

www.crossroadsconnect.com

www.davidcrowderband.com

www.epicreality.com

www.flickernail.com

www.giftcardgiver.com

www.ginkworld.com

www.growingleaders.com

www.growinguppink.com

www.imagodeicommunity.com

www.laurenwinner.net

www.marksanborn.com

www.mops.org

www.mosaic.com

www.next-wave.org

www.northpoint.org

www.risenmagazine.com

www.sportreach.org

www.thepackergroup.com

www.theportico.org

www.tribalgeneration.com

www.ubcwaco.org

www.undertheoverpass.com

www.valorieburton.com

www.velocityculture.com

www.vortexdownload.com

www.walkthru.org

www.x3watch.com

www.xxxchurch.com

The Catalyst Bookshelf
Must-Read's for the Next Gen Leader

We asked our Catalyst friends & family for their recommended "must reads" … check out what we found. Many of these resources were featured in, or served as inspiration for, this GroupZine™

Authentic in Influence

The Next Generation Leader
By Andy Stanley

Leadership 101
By John C. Maxwell

The 21 Irrefutable Laws of Leadership
By John C. Maxwell

The Leadership Challenge
By James Kouzes and Barry Posner

What's Really Holding You Back? Closing the Gap Between Where You Are and Where You Want to Be
By Valorie Burton

Spiritual Leadership
By Henry Blackaby

The Barbarian Way
By Erwin Raphael McManus

What Every CEO Wants You to Know
By Ram Charan

Leadership and Self Deception
By the Arbinger Institute

Developing the Leader Within You
By John C. Maxwell

Blink!
By Malcolm Gladwell

Tipping Point
By Malcolm Gladwell

Habitudes: The Art of Self Leadership
By Tim Elmore

Habitudes: The Art of Leading Others
By Tim Elmore

Uncompromising in Integrity

Integrity
By Stephen L. Carter

Like a Rock: Laying the Foundation for the Rest of Your Life
By Andy Stanley

A Life of Integrity
By Howard G. Hendricks

Choosing to Cheat
By Andy Stanley

The Best Question Ever
By Andy Stanley

Ethics 101
By John C. Maxwell

Fred Factor
By Mark Sanborn

Real Sex
By Lauren Winner

Passionate about God

Girl Meets God
By Lauren Winner

Mudhouse Sabbath
By Lauren Winner

A Tale of Three Kings: A Study in Brokenness
By Gene Edwards

Christ Plays in Ten Thousand Places: A Conversation in Spiritual Theology
By Eugene Peterson

What's so Amazing about Grace
By Philip Yancy

Experiencing God
By Henry Blackaby

Your God is Too Safe
By Mark Buchanan

The Ragamuffin Gospel
By Brennan Manning

Walking on Water
By Madeliene L'Engle

The Gospel According to Moses: What My Jewish Friends Taught Me About Jesus
by Athol Dickson

I Am Not But I Know I Am
By Louie Giglio

(Re)understanding Prayer
By Kyle Lake

NOOMA DVDs
By Rob Bell

Velvet Elvis
By Rob Bell

Dinner With a Perfect Stranger
By Davide Gregory

Intentional about Community

Urban Tribes
By Ethan Watters

How People Grow
By Henry Cloud & John Townsend

Community of Kindness
By Steve Sjogren & Rob Lewin

As Iron Sharpens Iron: Building Character
in a Mentoring Relationship
By Howard Hendricks

Jesus in the Margins
By Rick McKinley

An Unstoppable Force
By Erwin McManus

Creating Community: 5 Keys to Building a
Small Group Culture
By Andy Stanley & Bill Willits

Volunteer Revolution
By Bill Hybels

Love is the Killer App
By Tim Sanders

Relationships 101
By John C. Maxwell

25 Ways to Win With People
By John C. Maxwell and Les Parrott

Courageous in Calling

Wild at Heart
By John Eldredge

The Divine Conspiracy
By Dallas Willard

The Call: Finding and Fulfilling the Central
Purpose of Your Life
By Os Guinness

Holy Ambition: What It Takes to Make a
Difference for God
By Chip Ingram

The Search For Significance: Seeing Your
True Worth through God's Eyes
By Robert S. McGee

Blueprint for Life
By Ben Ortlip

Searching for God Knows What
By Donald Miller

The Purpose Driven Life
By Rick Warren

Chasing Daylight
By Erwin McManus

God's Blogs
By Lanny Donoho

Understanding God's Will
By Kyle Lake

Twenty Something
By Margaret Feinberg

The Purpose Driven Life
By Rick Warren

Epic
By John Eldredge

Engaged in Culture

The Christian in Today's Culture
By Chuck Colson and Nancy Pearcy

Ancient Future Evangelism
By Robert Webber

Revolution
By George Barna

The Emerging Church
By Dan Kimball

A New Kind of Christian
By Brian McLaren

Blue Like Jazz
By Donald Miller

Total Truth: Liberating Christianity from Its
Cultural Captivity
By Nancy R. Pearcey

Church in Emerging Culture: Five
Perspectives
*By Leonard Sweet, Andy Crouch, Michael
Horton, Frederica Mathewes-Green, Brian
McLaren, & Erwin Raphael McManus*

Out of the Question ... Into the Mystery
By Dr. Leonard Sweet

Summoned to Lead
By Dr. Leonard Sweet

Life@Work
*By John C. Maxwell, Thomas G.
Addington, & Stephen R. Graves*

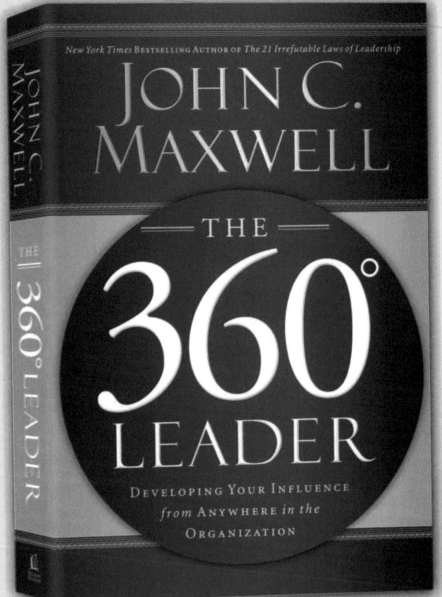

NELSON IMPACT

A Division of Thomas Nelson Publishers
Since 1798

The Nelson Impact Team is here to answer your questions
and suggestions as to how we can create more resources
that benefit you, your family, and your community.

Contact us at Impact@thomasnelson.com